THE LION
ENCYCLOPEDIA OF
World
Religions

DAVID SELF

LION

Text copyright © 2008 David Self
This edition copyright © 2008 Lion Hudson

The moral rights of the author have been asserted

A Lion Children's Book
an imprint of
Lion Hudson plc
Wilkinson House, Jordan Hill Road,
Oxford OX2 8DR, England
www.lionhudson.com
UK ISBN 978 0 7459 4983 3
US ISBN 978 0 8254 7852 9

First edition 2008
10 9 8 7 6 5 4 3 2 1

Typeset in 12/15 Latin 725 BT
Printed and bound in Hong Kong

Distributed by:
UK: Marston Book Services Ltd, PO Box 269, Abingdon, Oxon OX14 4YN
USA: Trafalgar Square Publishing, 814 N Franklin Street, Chicago, IL 60610
USA Christian Market: Kregel Publications, PO Box 2607, Grand Rapids, MI 49501

Acknowledgments
The author and Lion Hudson wish to thank the following people for their help
and advice:
Mary Hayward, Independent Educational Consultant
Professor Xinzhong Yao, Director, the Centre for Chinese Studies, University of Wales,
Lampeter
Dr Wendy Dossett, Lecturer in Religious Studies, University of Wales, Lampeter
Abdul Majid Jawad
Stephen Vickers
The author would also like to thank the designer, Emma DeBanks, and the editor,
Kirsten Etheridge, for their dedication, eye for detail, pursuit of consistency, patience
and understanding!

Text Acknowledgments
Bible extracts, unless otherwise stated, are taken or adapted from the Good News Bible,
published by The Bible Societies/HarperCollins Publishers Ltd, UK © American Bible
Society 1966, 1971, 1976, 1992.

The Apostle's Creed (on page 35) and the Lord's Prayer (on page 37) from Common
Worship: Services and Prayers for the Church of England (Church House Publishing,
2000) are copyright © The English Language Liturgical Consultation, 1988 and used
with permission.

Sources:
Chart on page 119: BBC website, figured modified October 2005.

Picture Acknowledgments
Every effort has been made to trace and contact copyright owners. We apologize for any
omissions or errors.
t=top, b=bottom, c=centre, l=left, r=right

David Alexander: pp. 8l; 12c/British Museum; 18c; 19t; 22l; 29t.
Susanna Burton: pp. 33; 36c; 49; 123cl.
Jacqueline Crawford: p. 7b.
Anthony Etheridge: p.10–11b.
Getty Images: pp. 1 and 105b/Neil Farrin/Asia Images;
7r/Kenneth Garrett/National
Geographic; 9r and 28l/Martin Gray/National Geographic; 10c and 31t/Altrendo Travel;
11r/Harald Sund/Photographer's Choice; 11t and 62l/Frans Lemmens/The Image Bank;
15b/Dorling Kindersley; 18–19b/Tom Stoddart Archive; 20l/Jewish School/Bridgeman Art
Library; 26t/David Silverman; 29b/Santi di Tito/Bridgeman Art Library; 32l/Bob
Thomas/Stone; 37t/Richard Koek/Stone; 39t/Terje Rakke/The Image Bank; 42b/China
Photos/Stringer; 42l/Giotto di Bondone/Bridgeman Art Library; 47l/Nakkas
Osman/Bridgeman Art Library; 47br/David Sutherland/Photographer's Choice; 48l/Chris

McGlashon/AFP; 51/Asif Hassan/AFP; 52br/Cecile Treal and Jean-Michel Ruiz/Dorling
Kindersley; 53b/Thomas Schmitt/Stone; 54–55b/Nabeel Turner/Stone; 57br/Bruno
Barbier/Robert Harding World Imagery; 59tl/Peter Kramer; 59b/Per-Anders Pettersson;
60b/Ursula Gahwiler/Robert Harding World Imagery; 65b/Indian School/Bridgeman Art
Library; 65t/Manan Vatsyayana/AFP; 69b/Tim Graham; 71cr/Robert Nickelsberg/Liaison;
72b/Paul Beinssen/Lonely Planet Images; 75b/Hilarie Kavanagh/Stone; 75t/Andrea
Pistolesi/Riser; 77b/Topical Press Agency; 79b/Robert Nickelsberg; 79c/Elena
Segatini/Stone; 81b and 82br/Angelo Cavalli/The Image Bank; 82t/Alison Wright/Robert
Harding World Imagery; 82bl/Martin Gray/National Geographic; 83b/Tai Power Seeff/The
Image Bank; 84/Richard I'Anson/Lonely Planet Images; 85t/Sena Vidanagama/AFP;
86b/Alison Wright/National Geographic; 87/Jeff Brass; 88l/Shoko Yukitake /Taxi;
93br/AFP; 99tr and 123bl/Narinder Nanu/AFP; 105t/STF/AFP; 109t/Liu Jin/AFP;
109b/China Photos; 111c/Gavin Hellier/Photographer's Choice; 112/Paul
Chesley/Photographer's Choice; 113t/Time Life Pictures/Mansell; 115b/Gavin Gough/The
Image Bank; 116b/Allan Tannenbaum/Time Life Pictures; 121b/David Silverman;
123tc/STR/AFP.
Lion Hudson: pp. 14 and 121t/David Townsend; 24; 40l; 41r.
Rex Nicholls: pp. 17; 35t.
Steve Rock: pp. 36l; 66; 68c; 76b; 83t; 88br; 110t; 111t; 117t; 122.
Nick Rous: p. 4–5b.
Toybox/Richard Hanson, 2007 (www.toybox.org): p. 43b.
Richard Watts: maps on pp. 13t, 16t, 28b, 30c, 47t, 55t, 60t, 76t, 86t, 118–119c;
graphics on pp. 4–5 (and thereafter), 80, 119t.

Picture research below courtesy of Zooid Pictures Limited.

akg-images: pp. 16/Erich Lessing; 41; 67/Archiv Gerstenbe/ullstein bild.
Alamy: pp. 5/Images of Africa Photobank; 22b and 28b/Israel images; 27c/Danita
Delimont; 40b/Barry Lewis; 44/North Wind Picture Archives; 50tl, 68t, 69c, 71b, 91t, 92,
94b and 97tr/ArkReligion.com; 52l/Picture Contact; 54tl, 78l, 89br and 94t/World
Religions Photo Library; 46/Tengku Mohd Yusof; 58/Mehdi Chebil; 61/Dinodia Images;
77t/David Bagnall; 85b/Richard Wareham; 89t/Robert Harding Picture Library Ltd;
97tl/Gerry Walden; 103t/Devinder Sangha; 110cl/Eitan Simanor; 113r/Oliver Benn;
116t/colinspics; 120t/J Marshall – Tribaleye Images; 123tl/Fabrice Bettex; 123tr/Henry
Westheim Photography; 123br/Tibor Bognar.
Ancient Art & Architecture Collection: p. 60l/Husain A. Afsar/Ancient Art &
Architecture Collection.
Arabian Eye: p. 45t.
Art Archive: pp. 8–9/Museo Nazionale Palazzo Altemps Rome/Dagli Orti.
Bodleian Library, University of Oxford: p. 30.
Bridgeman Art Library: pp. 15t/Giraudon; 35/University of Liverpool Art Gallery &
Collections, UK.
Christian Aid Photo Library: p. 38/Sarah Filbey.
Circa Photo Library: pp. 97b and 101b/John Smith.
Corbis UK Ltd: pp. 6 and 34/The Art Archive; 12–13/Cheryl Diaz Meyer/Dallas Morning
News; 20/Najlah Feanny; 21r/Claudia Kunin; 25t/David H. Wells; 25b/Pnc/Brand X;
31b/Atlantide Phototravel; 32b/Gleb Garanich/Reuters; 36–37/Pascal Deloche/Godong;
39r/Lars Halbauer/Dpa; 48b/Smithsonian Institution; 50bl/Lowell Georgia; 50tr and
50br/Image100; 56/Cesar Vera/Latinvisions; 59tr/DK Limited; 62–63/Christophe Boisvieux;
64t/Angelo Hornak; 64b/Historical Picture Archive; 69t and 73t/Jayanta Shaw/Reuters;
73b and 102l/Ajay Verma/Reuters; 74/Altaf Qadri/Epa; 78r/Paul Almasy; 81c/Galen
Rowell; 89bl/Tim Graham; 90/Lindsay Hebberd; 92b and 100b/Amit Bhargava; 95t and
103b/Desai Noshir Sygma; 106 and 107t/Archivo Iconografico, S.A.; 107b/Earl & Nazima
Kowall; 108t/Liu Liqun; 109b/China Photo/Reuters; 113l/Clay Perry; 115c/Hanan Isachar;
120b/Jason Reed/Reuters; 123cr/Leland Bobbè.
Getty Images: pp. 45b/Awad Awad/AFP; 54bl/Mohammed Abed/AFP; 57bl/China
Photos; 72t/Raveendran/AFP; 90–91/Martin Gray/National Geographic; 96, 98–99, 99tl
and 100t/Narinder Nanu/AFP; 101t/AFP; 117b/Carl De Souza/AFP.
Michael Holford: p. 81t.
Bury Peerless: p. 95b.
PA Photos: pp. 21l/Franka Bruns; 43t and 71t/Associated Press; 70t/Binod
Joshi/Associated Press; 70b/Ajit Solanki/Associated Press; 123bc/Manish
Swarup/Associated Press.
Reproduced with permission of the Bahá'í International Community: pp. 114;
115t.
Rex Features: pp. 23/Sipa Press; 25c/Yael Tzur.
Superstock Ltd: p. 104.
Capt Suresh Sharma Photography: p. 102r/Photographers Direct.
World Religions Photo Library: p. 92t/Christine Osborne.

Contents

For millions of people around the world, their religious faith is what helps them make sense of their lives.

The Symbols of the World Religions

HINDUISM
This symbol (said 'Om' or 'Aum') represents what cannot be imagined, Brahman.

JUDAISM
The 'menorah', or branched candlestick, is a symbol of both the Jewish faith and the state of Israel. The Star of David (one of the kings of the Jewish people) is also known as the 'Magen David' and is the oldest and most widely used symbol.

BUDDHISM
The eight-spoked wheel is the symbol of the Buddha's teaching.

CHRISTIANITY
The cross on which Jesus was put to death is a reminder for Christians of how Jesus died and rose again for all people. This is called his resurrection.

ISLAM
For people of hot desert countries who often travel by night when it is cool, the stars are their guide while the moon lights their way. Islam guides and lights its followers on the journey of life.

1 What is Religion?

'How did the world begin?' 'What is above the sky?' 'Who made the sun and the stars?' 'Who planned creation so that a tiny seed grows into a beautiful flower or into a crop that provides food?'

People have asked such questions for thousands of years. Nowadays, scientists provide some of the answers. That doesn't stop people asking, 'Who made the world?' Many have decided that it must all have been made by a special Being who existed before the universe was made.

Big Questions

The different religions of the world try to answer not only the question, 'How did the world begin?' They also try to answer questions such as, 'What happens when I die?' 'Why are we all here on earth?' and 'How can things be better?'

Many people find a religion gives meaning to their lives and gives them both help and strength. They are said to be 'religious'; they have faith. They may:

- read the holy books of their religion
- pray or meditate
- join other believers to worship
- give help to those who are in need.

Some religions owe their beginnings to one person; someone who first taught or revealed that particular faith – such as the Buddha, Jesus Christ, the Prophet Muhammad or Guru Nanak. Other religions have formed gradually over the centuries – such as Hinduism.

Some religions offer the hope of an everlasting life following life on earth. Others don't.

However they began and whatever their differences, they are important to their followers. To them they say, 'There is more to life than what we can see and touch. There is something holy that is greater than us.'

Creation Stories

The Hebrew Story

The ancient Hebrew people believed that 'in the beginning', God created the universe. He then created darkness and light. The next day he created the sky. On the following day, he created the seas and dry land – and then the plants. On the fourth day, he created the sun, moon and stars. On the fifth day, he created all the creatures that live in the sea and those that fly. On the sixth day, he created the animals and finally human beings. On the seventh, he rested.

This account appears in the first book of both the Jewish and Christian Bibles – called Genesis. It is also the teaching of the Qur'an, the Muslim holy book. Many Jews, Christians and Muslims believe that is exactly how it happened. Others believe that God did all this – but in a period longer than six days.

The Earthmaker

Native Americans told a story about the Earthmaker. He was always alone. It was always dark. He was lonely. He began to cry. He cried salt tears which flowed together to form the oceans. Out of those oceans grew life.

Unkulunkulu

The African Zulu people traditionally believed that the creator of everything was called Unkulunkulu or 'the Ancient One'. He came from the marshy reed beds and from them he grew the first people and the first cattle. He created the streams, the snakes and all the other animals. Then he taught the Zulu people how to hunt, how to make fire and how to grow food.

Look it Up

5 One God
29 Religions of the East
46 The Ten Gurus
54 Shinto (Creation)
58 Faith Around the World Today
60 Living Together

SIKHISM
The *Khanda* symbol shows a two-edged sword (the *khanda*) on a circle, flanked by two kirpans (or swords), and is a symbol of the Khalsa.

THE BAHÁ'Í FAITH
The symbol of the faith is a nine-pointed star.

CHINESE RELIGIONS
For Chinese people, the 'yin and yang' symbol means balance; each half contains the seed of the opposite.

SHINTO
The 'torii', or gateway, represents the entrance to a Shinto shrine.

JAINISM
In 1975, Jainism adopted the open palm as its symbol, a sign of peace. It often has the word 'ahimsa' (non-violence) written on it.

ZOROASTRIANISM
This symbol represents the *fravashi,* or guardian spirit; a sign that God is within people.

Ancient Egypt was a land of many gods and goddesses, the most important being the sun god.

The Sun God

'Where does the sun go at night?' 'Why does it seem to move across the sky?'

Like many early peoples, the ancient Egyptians worshipped the sun. It was their source of heat and light. It was the most important thing in their world.

The Egyptians named the sun god Re (sometimes spelled Ra). They believed that Re started on a journey every morning as a young man, moving across the sky. By midday, he was a full-grown, strong man. Towards evening, he got older and weaker until he died. During the night, he journeyed through a terrible underworld. But he was always reborn the next morning. For that, they gave thanks.

2 🌳 Ancient Egypt

The oldest known writing dates from around the year 3500 BCE. As a result of this, we know very little of the stories early humans told each other or of what they believed. Even so, we do know that 19,000 years ago people made paintings and carvings on the walls of the caves in which they lived. Some of these cave paintings show that early people thought that there were special beings who deserved respect: beings that are now called 'gods'.

One of the oldest religions that we know about was the religion of Ancient Egypt which flourished between the years 2500 BCE and 500 BCE. Although the Egyptians of that time did not write down the stories of their gods, we can work out some of what they believed from what is written in ancient burial places and on the remains of temples.

Some of these writings were carved into the walls of the burial places of the kings of Ancient Egypt. Each king (or 'pharaoh') was thought to be a son of the sun god, Re, and so the ancient Egyptians worshipped their pharaohs as well as Re and the other gods.

The Egyptian sun god, Re, shown journeying across the sky as if in a boat.

One God or Many?

One of the pharaohs of Ancient Egypt was called Amenhotep IV. He ruled in the early fourteenth century BCE and his wife was a beautiful woman called Nefertiti. He believed there was only one god, the sun god, Re.

Amenhotep changed his name to Akhenaten and closed all the temples to the other gods of Egypt. The name Akhenaten means 'spirit of Aten'. Aten was one name for the sun.

When he died, his young son Tutankhamun became king and he started to worship the other gods again.

Egypt in Later Times

By the year 300 BCE, Egypt had come under the power of the Greek empire. Later it came under Roman rule. During these periods, Egyptians honoured the Greek and Roman gods. Later still, Christianity became an important faith in Egypt. After 642 CE, the country became largely Muslim.

A statue of the goddess Bastet.

The Pyramids

The ancient Egyptians believed that a person's soul or spirit could not rest after death unless it could rest in its body. To stop the body decaying, it was preserved, or 'mummified', and buried with all the possessions it might need in an afterlife.

Pharaohs and other rich people had huge pyramid-shaped tombs built to be their resting places after death. Their mummified bodies were taken there by barge along the River Nile. One of the most famous tombs is that of Tutankhamun, which was discovered in 1922 CE.

Egyptian Gods

The Egyptian gods were thought to live in either the sky or an underworld beneath the earth. They were often pictured as humans with the heads of animals. Horus, the god of the sky, had the head of a falcon. Anubis, the god of the dead, had a jackal's head while Thoth (the moon god) had the head of an ibis.

Many animals, especially birds and cats, were thought to be god-like beings. For example, the goddess Bastet (who was a goddess of fertility and made crops grow along the River Nile) was always shown as a cat.

Look it Up

3 The Gods of Ancient Greece and Rome
5 One God

The gods of Ancient Greece and Rome were thought to take sides in human quarrels, wars and love affairs.

Religion

The word 'religion' comes from the Latin word *religio*. For the Romans (whose language was Latin), the word meant two things. First, it meant the bond or link between the gods and humans. Secondly, it meant the duty of humans to worship the gods.

Nowadays, the word 'religion' means a system of belief, often (but not always) linking humans and God, and often (but not always) involving worship.

The remains of the Parthenon, a temple to the Greek goddess Athena in Athens.

Look it Up

1 What is Religion?
14 The Spread of Christianity

3 🌳 The Gods of Ancient Greece and Rome

The Greeks believed there were many more gods and goddesses besides the twelve main ones (see panel right). Like humans, these gods were often jealous of one another. At other times they fought or fell in love. The Greeks told stories about them to try to explain why things (such as wars or earthquakes) happen in the world.

Stories of the gods were passed on by word of mouth. Eventually they were written down, most famously in two long poems called *The Iliad* and *The Odyssey*, both said to be written by a poet called Homer. In these long poems, human heroes take part in epic wars and travels, helped at times by different gods.

Worship of the Greek Gods

The Greeks built temples to honour their gods and goddesses. One of the most famous is the Parthenon in Athens, dedicated to the city's own goddess, Athena. At Delphi, there was a shrine dedicated to Apollo. There was also an oracle in Delphi (as in many other places). People visited these oracles to seek advice in times of need. At Delphi, the oracle took the form of a priestess who spoke words of wisdom believed to be given directly to her by Apollo for those who looked for help.

Many Greeks also had little shrines in honour of a particular god or goddess in their homes.

Gradually, belief in the Greek gods faded and the legends of the gods were seen as 'stories with a meaning' rather than historical events. This was due to the teaching of famous Greek thinkers such as Socrates.

The Religion of Rome

As the state of Rome conquered the lands around the Mediterranean Sea, it borrowed its religion from Greece – but gave their gods Roman names. The Romans believed these gods and goddesses protected the state of Rome and, later, the empire. Temples were built and special ceremonies were held to bring blessings on the empire or a particular city. The Romans also held festivals or holidays when prayers were said and ceremonies were performed by priests at the temples to please the gods.

The Roman religion did not teach people how to behave towards one another; nor did ordinary people visit the temples to worship the gods and goddesses. However, many Romans (like the Greeks) consulted oracles and many homes had shrines, where respect was paid especially to the goddess Vesta.

Because there was no need for ordinary people to visit the temples, the Romans at first allowed the peoples they ruled (such as the Jews) to worship in their own way. Later, they expected them to honour the Roman gods.

When some of the Roman emperors decided they themselves were gods, they demanded that all the peoples living in the Roman empire should worship them. Christians felt unable to do this and many were persecuted.

All this changed when the Roman emperor Constantine himself became a Christian – and worship of the Roman gods died away. Gradually, some of the Roman festivals were turned into Christian celebrations. For example, a Roman winter festival was chosen as the time when many Christians remember the birth of Jesus.

Roman stone carvings of the gods Jupiter, Pluto, Persephone (a goddess of the underworld), Neptune and Amphitrite (a sea goddess).

Remains of the temple to the god Apollo at Delphi in Greece.

The Olympians

The twelve main Greek gods were said to live on Mount Olympus, the highest mountain in Greece. The Romans later gave them new names (shown here in brackets).

Zeus, chief of the gods (Jupiter)

Hera, his wife and sister, goddess of marriage (Juno)

Apollo, son of Zeus and god of music, poetry and the sun (Apollo)

Athena, goddess of wisdom (Minerva)

Hermes, messenger of the gods (Mercury)

Poseidon, god of the seas (Neptune)

Artemis, goddess of hunting (Diana)

Ares, son of Zeus and Hera, god of war (Mars)

Aphrodite, goddess of love (Venus)

Hephaestus, god of fire and metal work (Vulcan)

Demeter, goddess of agriculture (Ceres)

Hestia, goddess of the home and hearth (Vesta)

Another Greek god named Hades or Pluto lived in and ruled the underworld.

Ancient, traditional faiths survive in many areas of the world.

Look it Up

The Dreamtime

The Aboriginal people of Australia believe their land was shaped in a distant past which they call the Dreamtime. Strange creatures, some of them giants, lived in the Dreamtime – and these beings are the ancestors of today's Aborigines.

When the ancestor-creatures journeyed across the earth, they made their mark on the landscape. Where a giant snake wriggled across the land, it became a river valley. Where a Dreamtime dingo curled up to rest, a deep hollow was formed. A giant emu egg became a rocky hill.

Stories from the Dreamtime are told from generation to generation and acted out in dances and rituals. Because the land was shaped by the Dreamtime spirits, Aborigines believe it should be treated with much respect.

Uluru – also known as Ayers Rock – in central Australia is a holy place for Aborigines.

4 🌳 Native Religions

In ancient times, before the great religions that are followed today spread around the world, local or native religions could be found in every part of the world. Each particular tribe might have its own beliefs, and worship its own special gods. In other areas, the same beliefs might be held by much larger groups of peoples.

The followers of these native religions may not have learned the art of writing but the stories they told from one generation to another showed their great respect for the power of nature and their understanding of the holiness of life.

When the religions of Christianity and Islam spread their beliefs around the world, many followers of native religions became Christian or Muslim. Their original beliefs either simply disappeared or were absorbed into Christian or Muslim teachings. Even so, native religions have survived in, for example, areas around the River Amazon and on some Indonesian islands; nor have they disappeared completely in Africa or India.

In other areas, they have gained new respect. At one time, the rulers of the United States of America tried to ban the beliefs and practices of Native Americans. Now there is support for their beliefs. In Australia, Aboriginal groups were once deprived of lands they believed to be holy. Their beliefs are also now granted more respect. Maori traditions in New Zealand have also survived into modern times.

A carving on the roof of a Maori meeting house in New Zealand.

The Spirit World

Native religions each have their own different beliefs but many of them teach that there is a spirit world. In this world live good spirits that can help humans and evil spirits that can send disasters into the world of humans.

The Great Spirit

Most Native Americans believe the world was created by a 'Great Spirit' who has many names. The Lakota Sioux Indians call the Spirit *Wakan Tanka*; the Iroquois use the name *Orenda*.

Besides the Great Spirit, Native Americans honour other guardian spirits which can be contacted with the help of a shaman – sometimes known as a 'medicine man' because he brings healing from the spirit world to humans.

Storytelling is very important to Native Americans, and the storyteller of a tribe (usually an older man or woman) is much respected. He or she keeps alive the tribe's ancient stories, many of which explain why the world is how it is.

Many of these stories involve animals. One tells how the cunning coyote (known as *Speel-yi*) tried to steal the light of the sun and moon. In his attempt, he let cold into the world. An Apache story tells how the coyote again tries to trick the sun by stealing tobacco from the sun – only to be tricked himself by the Apaches.

A South American shaman.

Followers of native religions often hold ceremonies (or dances or other rituals) in which they try to make contact with good spirits to bring blessings on the tribe or on a particular family – for example, to bring healing to a sick child. Other ceremonies may be held to frighten away evil spirits that might cause the failure of a harvest or a drought – or take possession of a human.

For this reason, special rituals are important in many native or tribal religions. So too is the belief that it is wrong to disturb or harm the natural world – as that would disturb the spirits of the land, trees and rivers.

In some native religions, men known as shamans have particular importance. Shamans are thought to have powers that allow them to make contact with the spirits and even visit the spirit world. Some shamans, especially in South America, eat mushrooms which put them in a trance during which they make such visits.

Native Americans proclaim their family history with tall wooden carvings known as totem poles.

5 🌳 One God

Although there now seem to be many differences between the Jewish, Christian and Muslim religions, they have much in common – including belief in one God. They also have their roots in the same part of the world. Jews, Christians and Muslims all teach that one of the 'fathers' of their faith was a man known as Abram, Abraham or Ibrahim. The name means 'father of many'.

For this reason, they are sometimes called the Ibrahamic faiths.

Monotheism

'Monotheism' is the belief that there is one and only one God, the God who brought all things into being and who, at the same time, cares for everyone.

We do not know for certain how this belief in monotheism came about. It could have happened in one of two ways:

• People originally believed in just one God. The Jewish and Christian Bibles begin with the story of God creating the first man, Adam, who (with his wife Eve) believed in the one God. Later, people came to worship many gods. Jews (and Christians) believe that it was the prophets (or teachers) who brought people back to the worship of one God. Muslims believe that it was the Prophet Muhammad who restored belief in one God.

• People originally believed in many gods. Gradually, various nations came to believe that one God (among many gods) was special to them – and, later still, came to believe that there is only one God.

Abraham

For Jews, Abraham is the founding father, or 'patriarch', of their nation and religion.

It is not known for certain when he was born but he is said to have lived near or in a city called Ur in a land then named Mesopotamia – what is now northern Iraq. Mesopotamia lay between the rivers Tigris and Euphrates. Its name means 'between two rivers'.

Abraham became unhappy with the way people of that region worshipped many gods and he followed what he believed was the call of the one true God to leave home.

A carving found near Ur, an ancient city said to be the birthplace of Abraham. This carving dates from around 2500 BCE.

The Shatt al Arab Waterway, where the rivers Euphrates and Tigris meet near Basra in what is now Iraq.

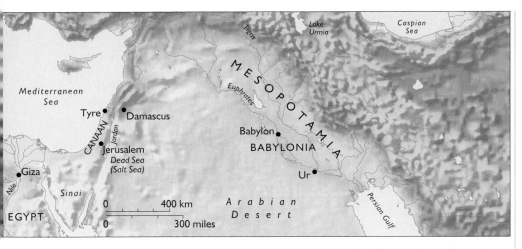

The world of Abraham, sometimes known as the Fertile Crescent because it stretches from the River Jordan round to the mouth of the Euphrates (in the Persian Gulf).

He became a wanderer, or 'nomad', moving west to a land known as Canaan.

Genesis, the first of the Jewish and Christian holy books, tells how God made an agreement, or 'covenant', with him that God would give that land ('a land flowing with milk and honey') to his children, who became known as the Jewish people. They are also known as the 'Children of Israel' because Abraham's grandson Jacob later became known as Israel.

Christians honour Abraham as a faithful and good man who was obedient to God at all times – especially in obeying God's call to leave Mesopotamia and in being ready to sacrifice his son Isaac.

For followers of Islam, he is the 'first Muslim' and is known as Ibrahim (the Arabic version of the name Abraham). Along with Moses, Ibrahim is the most frequently mentioned Prophet in the Qur'an. The Qur'an says that Ibrahim rejected the worship of the sun, moon and stars, and turned to the one creator God.

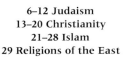

Look it Up

6–12 Judaism
13–20 Christianity
21–28 Islam
29 Religions of the East

The Sacrifice

Abraham once heard God speaking to him, ordering him to take his only son Isaac (Ishaq in Arabic) to a mountain. There, he was to sacrifice Isaac as a gift to God. (In those days, people would sacrifice an animal over a fire as a gift to honour God.) Because Abraham was obedient to God, he was prepared even to sacrifice his son – so he loaded wood for the fire onto a donkey.

Abraham and Isaac set off towards the distant hillside. As they climbed the hill, Abraham carried a knife and live coals to start the fire and Isaac carried the wood. Isaac asked where the lamb for the sacrifice was. Abraham replied that God would provide one.

When they reached the place, Abraham prepared the fire, tied up his son and put his hand on his knife. At that very moment, as Abraham was about to carry out the deed, he heard a voice. He turned round and saw a sheep caught in a bush. 'Abraham,' said the voice, 'kill this sheep in the place of Isaac, for you have proved you are a loyal and faithful servant. I am very pleased with you.' Abraham realized then that God had been testing him and had never wanted the death of Isaac.

JUDAISM

For Jews, Moses is 'God's servant' and their greatest leader.

6 ♆ Moses and the Exodus

Mount Sinai.

Mount Sinai

While the Israelites were in the desert, Moses is said to have climbed a mountain, Mount Sinai. There he is said to have met God.

Jews believe that it was on Mount Sinai that God gave Moses the Ten Commandments, written on tablets of stone, and other laws. For centuries, the Jews kept these in a special chest or case known as the 'ark of the covenant'.

Jews also believe that, on Mount Sinai, an agreement, or 'covenant', was established between God and his 'chosen people': God would guard and protect them as long as they followed God's laws. The ark of the covenant was a sign of God's presence with his people.

According to the holy writings of Judaism, God promised to Abraham and all his descendants that, one day, they would have their own land. At this time, they were known as the Israelites or Hebrews. Before they could settle in Canaan, their 'Promised Land', they were forced to live as slaves in Egypt. Jewish scriptures tell how they had moved there in a time of famine, in the hope of finding food.

In Egypt, the Israelites were forced to do much heavy building work and suffered in many ways – but God promised he would lead them out of Egypt and into their own land. Eventually, one of them, a man called Moses, became their leader and spokesman.

A number of plagues began to affect Egypt. After each one struck, Moses spoke to the Egyptian ruler (thought to be the pharaoh Rameses II) promising that Egypt would suffer no more if he let the Israelites leave the country. Each time, Rameses agreed, only to go back on his word when that particular plague ended.

One night, many Egyptian boys died. The Jewish scriptures describe how, that night, death 'passed over' the homes of the Israelites and none of their sons died. This time the pharaoh granted the Israelites permission to leave Egypt – which they did. This event is known as the Exodus.

Under Moses' leadership, the Israelites spent the next 40 years as nomads, wandering in the Sinai desert before eventually reaching the 'Promised Land' about which God had spoken to Abraham.

Pesach

Jews continue to celebrate the Passover each year with a festival called 'Pesach'. They have a special meal that begins with the question, 'Why is this night different from all other nights?'

The answer is because it marks their escape from Egypt – an event said to have happened over 3,000 years ago.

Jews remember their escape with this 'Passover meal' or 'Seder', which means 'order'. They eat the meal at home. All the family and many friends are invited. The best cloth and best dishes are placed on the table. There is a wine glass for everyone, including the children. In the middle of the table is the Seder plate.

Egyptian slaves building a wall.

The meal begins with the father of the family saying a prayer, dipping parsley in salt water and giving it to everyone. He then breaks a 'matzah' in two and shares one piece among everyone. Then the youngest child has to ask the question, 'Why is this night different from all other nights?'

And the father tells the story of the escape from Egypt.

The Seder Plate

On the Seder plate, special foods are arranged as a reminder of the festival's meaning:

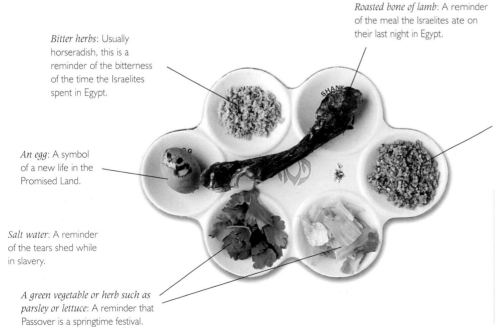

Roasted bone of lamb: A reminder of the meal the Israelites ate on their last night in Egypt.

Matzot: Wafers of unleavened bread are a reminder that the Israelites left Egypt in such a hurry they did not have time to bake proper bread to take with them.

Bitter herbs: Usually horseradish, this is a reminder of the bitterness of the time the Israelites spent in Egypt.

Haroset: A mixture of apples, nuts, cinnamon spice and wine: it is both a symbol of freedom and a reminder of the mortar the Israelites used when making bricks for the Egyptians.

An egg: A symbol of a new life in the Promised Land.

Salt water: A reminder of the tears shed while in slavery.

A green vegetable or herb such as parsley or lettuce: A reminder that Passover is a springtime festival.

Look it Up

5 One God
7 The Promised Land
8 The Tenakh
9 Home and Synagogue

The story of the Jewish people centres on the story of the land promised to Abraham.

A Philistine warrior.

The Story of David and Goliath

One of the Philistines was a giant of a man called Goliath, said to be nearly three metres tall. He challenged any Israelite to take him on in single combat. The outcome was to decide who won the battle.

A young Israelite called David heard of the challenge. He went to the Israelites' king, Saul, and volunteered – convinced God would protect him. When Goliath saw David approaching, he just laughed.

David stopped, still some distance away from Goliath. He took a pebble, put it in his sling and took aim. The pebble hit Goliath straight on the forehead with such force it knocked him unconscious and he fell to the ground. David ran towards him, seized the huge man's sword and, with it, killed him.

7 ☿ The Promised Land

Despite having been led by Moses to Canaan (their 'Promised Land'), the Israelites still had to defend themselves from frequent attacks, even though they had no proper army. Their soldiers were mostly farmers who had joined together to try to defend their land, relying mainly on wooden clubs and slingshots (a leather cup which could be whirled round to catapult a stone at an object up to 50 metres away).

Many of the attacks on the Israelites came from a people known as the Philistines (who had chariots and proper armour). They had settled along the coast of Canaan. From them comes another name for this area: Palestine.

The kingdoms of Judah and Israel from 933 BCE onwards.

The Kingdom

A holy man of God called Samuel realized the Israelites needed to be united to defeat the Philistines so, in approximately 1025 BCE, he crowned a man called Saul as king of the Israelites. It was during Saul's reign that the boy called David defeated Goliath.

Eventually Saul was killed in battle by the Philistines and David became king. He made Jerusalem his capital city, had the ark of the covenant brought there and built himself a palace in the city. On his death, his son Solomon became king. He was famous for his wealth and wisdom and for completing the first Temple in Jerusalem – in which was kept the ark. As Solomon's wealth came from heavy taxation, he became unpopular. After his death (about 933 BCE), the 'Promised Land' became two countries.

Israel

The northern part of Canaan became known as Israel. Its capital was Samaria. One of its greatest prophets was Elijah – who was never afraid to tell the king of Israel when he was doing wrong.

In 721 BCE, Israel was defeated by a people called the Assyrians. Many Israelites were taken captive. Those who remained married Assyrians. Very much later, the people living in this area became known as Samaritans.

Judah

The southern kingdom lasted longer but gradually its people began to ignore their religion and its laws. A prophet called Jeremiah warned them that Jerusalem (which remained the capital of Judah) would be destroyed as a punishment for their wrongdoing.

In 596 BCE, the king of Babylon, Nebuchadnezzar, attacked Judah, and the Jews (as the people of Judah became known) were forced to surrender; 10,000 were taken back to Babylon (in what is now Iraq) as captives. Nine or ten years later, the remaining Jews rebelled against Babylonian rule and Jerusalem was completely destroyed.

The Return

Some years later, Babylon was in turn defeated – by nations known as the Medes and Persians – and the Jews were given their freedom. Some chose to stay in Babylon. Many returned and set about rebuilding their city and the Temple.

Five hundred years later, this tiny country was conquered yet again – first by the Greeks and later by the Romans. The Romans allowed the Jews to follow their religion and way of life until the year 70 CE. The Jews were then exiled from their 'Promised Land' until their homeland was returned to them in 1947.

Look it Up

5 One God
6 Moses and the Exodus
9 Home and Synagogue
12 Judaism in the Modern World
59 Religious Conflict

The Temple

The first Temple in Jerusalem lasted from the time of Solomon until Jerusalem was destroyed by the Babylonians in 586 BCE.

The building of its replacement began around 520 BCE. Five hundred years later, King Herod (who was king at the time of the birth of Jesus) began to enlarge it. It was known as the Second Temple or Herod's Temple. Enormous in size, it occupied one sixth of the city.

This Temple was destroyed by the Romans in 70 CE, and all that remains is the Western Wall. Even so, Jerusalem continues to be the focus of all Jewish worship. All synagogues face towards Jerusalem.

The city of Jerusalem in the first century CE.
The Temple was built on the orders of King Herod.

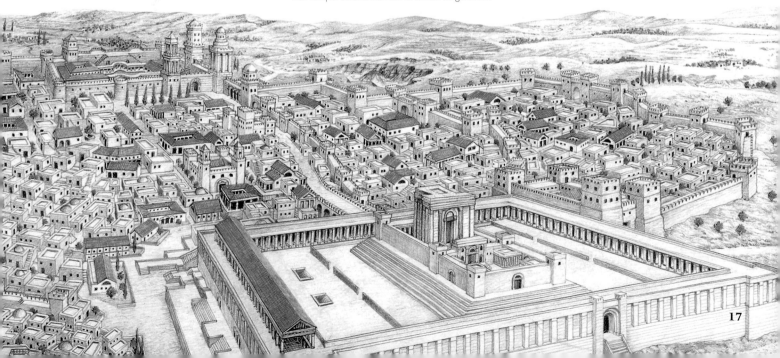

The *Tenakh* is not one book but many and is the most important of all the Jewish holy writings.

The Psalms

These holy songs are often called 'the Psalms of David' because he was a skilled singer and player of the lyre – but he was not necessarily their author. Many could, however, have been written from his experiences.

Before becoming king, David had looked after his father's sheep. He might easily have thought that, just as he was their shepherd, so God was his people's shepherd. This is how Psalm 23 begins:

The Lord is my shepherd,
I shall not want.
He makes me lie down in green
pastures,
He leads me beside still waters,
He restores my soul.

Orthodox Jewish boys study printed copies of the Torah.

Look it Up

6 Moses and the Exodus
9 Home and Synagogue
10 What Does it Mean to Be Jewish?

8 ♈ The Tenakh

Among the Jewish holy books is a collection of 24 books which are known as the Jewish 'Bible' or *Tenakh*. This Hebrew word comes from the initial letters (T-N-K) of the three groups of books that make up the Jewish Bible. It was first written in Hebrew, the language of the Jewish people, and many Jews still read it in the original language.

The Torah

The first five books of the *Tenakh* are known as the Torah or Pentateuch. They describe the early history of the Jewish people (or Israelites) up until the time they were eventually led towards the land that God had promised to Abraham: the Promised Land.

For Jews, the Torah is their most important holy scripture: the word *torah* means 'teaching' or 'Law' and includes the Ten Commandments and many rules about diet and behaviour.

The Torah, often written on long scrolls of parchment, is read in Jewish worship. Here, a boy carries a rolled-up Torah scroll in its elaborate case.

Orthodox Jews believe that these laws state how life should be lived for all time. Progressive or Liberal Jews believe that God continues to show his people how to live and that each generation must work out how to follow his law.

The Nevi'im

The *Nevi'im* or 'Prophets' can be subdivided into two groups of books: the history books, which tell the story of the Jewish people after their return from Egypt; and those books which record the teachings of the later prophets. These prophets were holy men who spoke of what God wanted his people to do and who warned them not to disobey God's commandments.

The Ketuvim

The *Ketuvim* or 'Writings' contains books of poetry, songs, stories and teachings. One book is the Book of Psalms, the sacred songs of the Jewish people.

Tefillin

Tefillin, also known as phylacteries, are little leather boxes containing short extracts from the Torah.

In one book of the Torah, Deuteronomy, Jews are told to bind them on their arms and wear them on their foreheads as a 'reminder' – so they do not forget the Law (Deuteronomy 6:8). Many Jews put them on at morning prayers and wear them every weekday.

The Ten Commandments

One of the books in the Torah, Exodus, tells how God is said to have given the Ten Commandments to Moses. The first four are about loving and honouring God; the rest are about respecting other people. Here is a summary of them:

1 You shall have no other gods but me.
2 You shall not make for yourself any idol.
3 You shall not dishonour the name of the Lord your God.
4 Remember the Lord's day and keep it holy.
5 Honour your father and mother.
6 You shall not murder.
7 You shall not commit adultery.
8 You shall not steal.
9 You shall not be a false witness.
10 You shall not covet anything which belongs to your neighbour.

Exodus 20:3–17

The first of these commandments was a reminder to the Jews not to behave like other peoples around them who believed in many gods.

The Talmud

There are other important Jewish writings, including the Talmud, which is a collection of laws, proverbs, parables and even jokes.

Jews believe God can be worshipped anywhere.

A Prayer at the Doorway

Many Jewish homes have a small box fixed to the right-hand side of the front doorpost. It contains a 'mezuzah' (plural mezuzot), a small piece of parchment on which is handwritten the *Shema*, one of the most important Jewish prayers. It begins: 'Hear O Israel! The Lord is our God, the Lord alone…' It ends: 'You shall inscribe them on the doorposts of your home and on your gates.'

A collection of mezuzot.

9 Home and Synagogue

There is a traditional Jewish riddle: 'Where does God live?' The answer is: 'Anywhere man lets him.' Although Jews go to a synagogue to worship God, they also feel that their homes are holy and special places where God can be worshipped.

The Home

For Jewish people, the home is a very special place. It is here that the holy day, the sabbath or 'Shabbat', begins. This weekly day of rest starts a little before sunset on Friday evenings and goes on till sunset the next evening. (For Jewish people, all days begin at sunset.)

The home is also a place where the mother of the family is particularly important. There is a Jewish saying: 'Whatever blessing dwells in the home comes from the wife.'

Tradition links Shabbat with the story of the creation of the world told in Genesis, the first book of the Bible. In that story, God rested on the seventh day – and so Shabbat is a day of rest, of worship and of study. It begins with the woman of the house lighting at least two candles and saying a prayer. Then, before the evening meal, the father of the family performs a ceremony called 'kiddush'. He takes a cup of wine (which is a symbol of joy) and says a blessing over it. Everyone drinks from the cup. The father then blesses the day, his wife and his children. The meal itself then begins with the blessing of two special loaves of bread called 'challot' (or *hallot*).

Because Shabbat is a day of rest (which means no work at all must be done during it), all the meals are prepared in advance. Some Jews, who follow the laws written in the Torah very strictly, will not (for example) answer a telephone or use their car on the sabbath. Others will drive only to the synagogue.

A Jewish family celebrates the Shabbat.

Shabbat service at the Pestalozzistrasse Synagogue in Berlin, Germany.

The Synagogue

Synagogues (in some parts of the world called 'temples' or 'shuls') are not only places for worship and prayer. They are meeting places for the local Jewish community: they are a kind of second home. They may be no larger than a room; others can seat several hundred. Some also have classrooms, a hall and a kitchen.

The most important part of the synagogue is the Holy Ark, a kind of cupboard set in the wall at the Jerusalem-facing end of the synagogue. In it are kept the scrolls on which the Torah is handwritten in Hebrew. The Ark is named after the chest in which the Jews once kept the tablets believed to be given by God to Moses. In the synagogue, the Ark is usually covered by a curtain and above it hangs a lamp. Known as 'the Eternal Light', it burns all the time as a reminder that God is always present. Near the Ark are two tablets with Hebrew letters on them, indicating the first words of the Ten Commandments.

In the centre of the synagogue is a platform called the *bimah*. It is from here that the Torah is read to the congregation. All the seats face the *bimah*. It is in the centre in Orthodox synagogues, but in Progressive synagogues it is placed in front of the Ark.

Jews visit their synagogue on important days in the year and also on the sabbath. Men cover their heads during worship as a mark of respect. In Orthodox synagogues, women sit apart from the men (often in an upstairs gallery). In most Progressive synagogues, everyone sits together.

The leader or minister of a congregation is usually a specially trained man (or, in some Progressive synagogues, a woman) called a 'rabbi' or teacher.

Reading the Torah

During the sabbath service, one of the Torah scrolls is usually carried round the synagogue and people reach out to touch it as a sign that they love the Torah. Sometimes the scrolls have little bells on them which tinkle as they are carried around.

Later, the scroll is taken to the *bimah* and its cover is taken off and it is opened. When people read from it, they do not touch it but use a pointer called a *yad* to follow the words. After the reading, someone holds the scroll up high for everyone to see.

It is a great honour to be asked to read from the Torah in a synagogue.

Look it Up

6 Moses and the Exodus
7 The Promised Land
8 The Tenakh
10 What Does it Mean to Be Jewish?

**Special customs
mark each stage
of Jewish life.**

An Orthodox Jew praying at the Western Wall.

Orthodox and Progressive

Like many religions, Judaism has followers who believe slightly different things. The two main groups are Orthodox Jews and Progressive Jews.

Orthodox Jews live very strictly by the Torah, keeping to its laws in detail. They wear special clothes for synagogue – where the language used is always Hebrew.

Progressive Jews feel that if a law seems to be out of date, it need no longer be observed. In most Progressive synagogues, men and women sit together and the service will be in the local language.

Look it Up

8 The Tenakh
9 Home and Synagogue
12 Judaism in the Modern World

10 🕎 What Does it Mean to Be Jewish?

Bar Mitzvah and Bat Mitzvah

One of the most important laws of Judaism is for all baby boys to be circumcised. That is, to have their foreskin removed. This ceremony (known as *bris, brit milah* or *berit milah*) happens on the eighth day of the boy's life. At the same time, the baby's name is announced.

A Jewish boy becomes an adult on his thirteenth birthday when he becomes 'bar mitzvah' ('son of the Law'), while a Jewish girl becomes 'bat mitzvah' ('daughter of the Law') a year earlier on her twelfth birthday.

Up till these birthdays, they have been learning the laws of God: what is right and what is wrong. When they become adults, their behaviour becomes their own responsibility.

Many of a boy's family and friends will go to the synagogue on the sabbath following the boy's birthday. This is the first time he will have taken an active part in a synagogue service. He says a prayer before the Torah is read and may read or chant a portion of Torah prescribed for that day. Many members of the family and friends will attend his bar mitzvah. Later there will be a special meal or party.

In Progressive synagogues, bat mitzvah happens just like bar mitzvah. Not all Orthodox synagogues have special ceremonies for this occasion. If they do, they will not take place during a synagogue service.

A Jewish girl, using a *yad*, reads from the Torah during her bat mitzvah in a Progressive synagogue.

A Jewish bride and groom celebrate under the wedding canopy.

Marriage

Jews are expected to get married – and many Jews believe it is important to marry someone who is also Jewish.

The wedding is normally held in a synagogue but in Israel it may take place outdoors. The bride and bridegroom stand under a special canopy called a *huppah*, a symbol of the home they will share together.

The rabbi who leads the wedding service says prayers over a glass of wine which he then gives to the bride and groom to drink. There are more prayers and then, at the end of the service, the bridegroom steps on the wine glass and breaks it. This is a sign or admission that there will be bad times as well as good during a marriage.

Death

Jews believe that, when a person dies, the funeral should happen as quickly as possible and the body should be buried within 24 hours. Cremation (the burning of the body) is not allowed in Judaism because Jews believe that it is the destruction of something precious made by God.

Kosher

Jews have many laws about which foods they can eat, as laid out in Deuteronomy 14. For example, they are not allowed to eat meat and dairy products (such as cheese) at the same meal.

Most Jews will eat only kosher food. The word 'kosher' (sometimes written *kasher*) means 'fit' or 'proper' and refers to foods permitted to be eaten. All fruits and vegetables are kosher but only certain kinds of meat and fish are. For example, pigs are 'forbidden' or 'trefa'. So are shellfish. Sheep, cattle, salmon, trout and haddock (for example) are all kosher. But even kosher animals (such as sheep and cattle) eaten must be killed in a special way with as little cruelty as possible.

Jews are told in the Torah to be kind to animals. At mealtimes, farm animals and pets should be fed first. Hunting is forbidden and no animal may be killed in front of its mother or baby.

Amen

One Hebrew word has entered almost every language of the world. It is used not only in Jewish worship but also at the end of many Christian and Muslim prayers. It is the word 'Amen', which means 'so be it' or 'yes, that is so'.

Many festivals of the Jews mark events in their history.

The Jewish Calendar

This calendar is based on the movement of the moon, so Jewish months have either 29 or 30 days. As these add up to only 354 days, every few years a thirteenth month is added to keep the Jewish year in step with the seasons of the 365-day-long 'Western', or solar, year. Even so, the dates in the Western calendar of Jewish holy days vary.

Jewish tradition says that the world was created in the year 3760 BCE and numbers years from that date. The Western year 2000 CE was therefore 5760 in Jewish numbering.

A shofar horn, blown at the start of the Days of Awe.

Look it Up

11 ♈ Jewish Holy Days

Five of the festivals celebrated in Judaism are described as 'major' because they are laid down in the Torah. Two of these mark a time for serious thought. They are Rosh Hashanah and Yom Kippur, and occur in the 'Days of Awe'. The other three, known as the Pilgrim Festivals, are Pesach, Shavuot and Sukkot.

The sabbath is celebrated as 'the queen of festivals' every week.

Days of Awe

These holy days begin with **Rosh Hashanah** (mid September). This is the start of the Jewish New Year and begins on a sabbath (Friday) evening with the mother of each family lighting candles in the home. During the meal, people eat pieces of apple dipped in honey in the hope that the new year will be sweet and prosperous.

It is said that, on this day, God opens the 'Book of Life' in which are written everyone's names, along with their good and bad deeds, and decides how they should be punished or rewarded. Rosh Hashanah is a solemn time for thinking about judgment. The word *rosh* means 'head' or 'beginning' and *hashanah* means 'year'.

In synagogues, a horn or 'shofar' is blown to start the ten-day period known as the Days of Awe – a period of 'making peace' with God.

Yom Kippur, the Day of Atonement, brings these days to an end. It begins with an evening service at which a special prayer called the 'Kol Nidrei' is said or sung three times. Jews fast for 25 hours and spend much of the day in their synagogue, confessing their sins and praying for forgiveness.

The Pilgrim Festivals

The most important of these is **Pesach**, which celebrates the Exodus from Egypt.

Sukkot

Immediately after Yom Kippur comes a period of celebration. **Sukkot** reminds Jews of the time they spent in the desert after leaving Egypt, when they slept in temporary huts known as *sukkot*. At this time of year, each Jewish family builds their own 'sukkah' from leaves and branches. They are often decorated with fruit. Depending on the climate, Jews either sleep in it for a week or just eat their meals in it.

The last day of this week-long festival celebrates what is traditionally the happiest of Jewish holidays. It is called Simchat Torah, which means 'rejoicing in the Torah'.

A Jewish sukkah in New York, USA.

The Torah is read in all synagogues over the course of a year, starting and ending on Simchat Torah – so, on this day, the last chapter of the fifth book (Deuteronomy) and the first chapter of the first book (Genesis) are both read to show that God's Law has no end but lasts for ever.

Lesser Festivals
Hanukkah (December)

Sometimes spelled Chanukah, this eight-day Jewish festival marks a time when the Jewish homeland was occupied by Syria. One man, Judas, became a leader of the resistance. He was nicknamed Maccabee ('the hammerer'). He and his followers made a number of raids, 'hammering' the Syrian army. Eventually he led his men into Jerusalem and set about cleansing the Temple.

Lighting the *hanukiah*, the Hanukkah lamp.

He lit the special lamp that was meant always to burn there, even though there was only enough oil for one day. Miraculously, it burned eight days until more oil was available. Jews still say in memory of those eight days, 'A great miracle happened here.' The Jewish word for 'dedication' is *hanukkah*.

Purim (March/April)

This spring festival celebrates the story of how a young Jewish woman called Esther saved her people from persecution when they had been taken into exile in Persia.

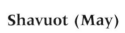

Children celebrate Shavuot.

Shavuot (May)

Shavuot celebrates the first fruits of the harvest and also the giving of the Law to Moses.

Synagogues are decorated with lilies and other flowers, as well as sheaves of corn or barley. The people eat dairy products at this time as a reminder that they had been promised their new home would be a land 'flowing with milk and honey'. Nowadays, a favourite food is cheesecake.

Shavuot occurs seven weeks (or 'a week of weeks') after Passover and is sometimes called Pentecost.

Jews have suffered greatly in the last 2,000 years.

Being Jewish

Jews say that you are Jewish if your mother is Jewish. You don't have to be religious. This means that those people born Jewish but who do not follow the religion are still counted as Jews.

Anyone who believes in God in the way that Judaism teaches and who keeps Jewish traditions can become Jewish – although Jews don't set out to persuade people to become Jewish. 'Being Jewish' means either that you follow the teachings of Judaism, or that you were born Jewish.

Modern Israel was created as a homeland for the Jewish people – but not everyone who lives in Israel is Jewish.

Throughout history, an important part of being Jewish has been to care for all forms of life. Many rabbis taught that the death penalty (even for murder) was wrong – long before other nations decided this. Jewish law teaches that cruelty to animals is wrong.

Look it Up

12 ♆ Judaism in the Modern World

The Romans who ruled the Jews' homeland at the time of Jesus originally allowed the Jews to follow their own religion and customs. Later, they became stricter and crueller in the way they treated the Jews. Finally, in the year 70 CE, they destroyed the Temple in Jerusalem.

To save their lives, most Jews fled from their 'Promised Land'.

Persecution

In the following centuries, the Jews had no homeland – and suffered continuing persecution. That is, they were made to suffer for their religion. They were not allowed to live in some countries. For example, in the year 1290 CE, all Jews were made to leave England. They were not allowed back for several centuries.

In those countries where they were allowed to settle, they were often ill-treated. Christian countries were often the worst places for Jews to live. In some cities, they were forced to live in certain areas which were kept locked at night. These areas were called 'ghettos'.

In Spain, in the year 1492 CE, Spanish Jews were given a choice. They could either become Christians or leave the country. Thousands left but some stayed and pretended to become Christian. When they were found out, Christians put them on trial. If they were found guilty, they were tortured and then put to death.

The Holocaust

Between 1937 and 1945, the Nazis (who then ruled Germany) treated Jews savagely. Jews in Germany were made to wear a yellow 'Star of David' on their clothing, so that it was obvious they were Jews. They were not allowed:

- to own cars
- to ride on buses or trains
- to be outside after 9pm
- to send their children to school.

Eventually, the Nazis decided they wanted to get rid of the Jews completely. They were rounded up and sent to prisons called concentration camps. Many were killed at once. Some were starved to death. Many were gassed. In all, the Nazis killed 6 million Jews. One and a half million of them were children. This event became known as the Holocaust. Since 1951, it has been remembered on 'Holocaust Day' each year. The day occurs during April or early May and, in Israel, all places of entertainment remain closed.

An Israeli schoolboy (wearing a yellow Star of David just as Jews were made to do by the German Nazis) lights candles in memory of the 6 million Jews put to death by the Nazis during a Holocaust Memorial Day ceremony.

A street within the 'Old City' area of modern Jerusalem.

Israel

In 1947, the Jews were once again given their own homeland when the country of Israel was created. This new state (which came into being in 1948) did not occupy all of what the Jews originally called their Promised Land. Since then, many Israelis have felt they should own all that land. This has been the cause of many conflicts between Jews and various Arab nations – as has the fact that the land that forms the state of Israel had previously been an Arab country called Palestine. In recent times, there has been much fighting between the Palestinians and the Israelis.

Although Jews have been given their homeland, many Jews still live in other countries around the world, including countries in Europe, America and parts of Africa.

The Western Wall

For Jews, Jerusalem is the centre of their 'Promised Land' – where King David built his capital city. All that remains of the Temple is its Western Wall, and many Jews hope that one day they will be able to go and pray there.

Many do this and there are usually crowds there on Shabbat evening (Friday night) and on the sabbath itself when Shabbat services are held there. Those who pray there often put small pieces of paper with their own special prayers written on them into the cracks between the stones, hoping that they will quickly reach God.

Men and women gather to celebrate Sukkot at the Western Wall.

Christianity began with one man, a Jew called Jesus.

An icon (or holy painting) of Mary the mother of Jesus with her son.

Son of God

Christians believe that Jesus Christ was fully human and experienced the pains and joys of life in the same way as other people – but they also believe that he was the Son of God.

By this, they mean that, although Mary was his mother, his father was God himself. Jesus was not only a human being, but God living on earth. They believe God became a man, suffered, died and then rose from the dead to save human beings from the results of their wrongdoings (or 'sins') and to promise them life after death.

The word 'Christ' is not a name but a title. It means 'the anointed' in Greek: the one who is chosen. The Hebrew word for this is 'Messiah'.

13 ✝ The Man Called Jesus

Christianity began about 2,000 years ago when a man called Jesus began teaching and healing in his Jewish homeland. Later, he became unpopular with some religious leaders and was put to death by being nailed to a wooden cross. His followers believe that, three days later, he rose from the dead. They call this event the resurrection.

Out of his life and teachings has grown Christianity – now the largest religion in the world.

The Life of Jesus

Historians agree that Jesus was a real person but, apart from what was written about him by his own followers, we know very little about him.

From those accounts, we know that he was born to a Jewish mother in a town called Bethlehem, six miles (ten kilometres) south of Jerusalem. Bethlehem was the home town of Mary's husband, Joseph. Jesus' parents were there to take part in a census. Their home was further north, in a town called Nazareth.

Jesus grew up in Nazareth. As he grew up, he went to the synagogue. Like Joseph, he probably worked as a carpenter or builder. When he was about 30, he chose twelve local men to be his closest followers or 'disciples'. He spent three years journeying around the country with them, teaching the people he met.

Large crowds came to listen. Some brought friends or relatives who were ill or disabled and Jesus helped or cured many of these people. These acts have come to be known as miracles.

Many people who heard him wondered if he might lead a revolution against the Romans who governed the country at this time.

Some of the Jewish religious leaders also began to see him as a threat and plotted to have him arrested. They got their chance

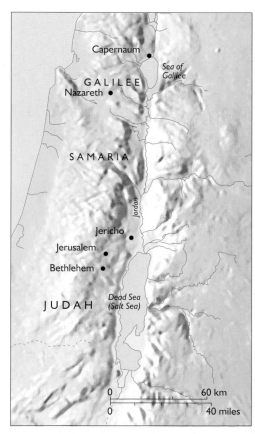

The land where Jesus lived.

when Jesus and his disciples went to Jerusalem to celebrate the Passover festival.

Jesus entered Jerusalem a few days before the festival (an event now remembered by Christians on Palm Sunday). On the Thursday evening, he had a last supper with his disciples (remembered in the Christian service of Holy Communion). Later that night he was betrayed by one of his twelve disciples, Judas. He was arrested, put on trial by the priests and, next morning, sent to the Roman governor, Pontius Pilate.

To prevent a riot, Pilate condemned him to death by crucifixion. Jesus died on the cross. For Christians, this is not the end of the story. They believe that three days later he rose from the dead and was seen and touched by his followers. After 40 days, he returned to his Father in heaven.

The death and resurrection of Jesus is remembered by Christians at Easter.

The River Jordan near Aenon, Salim, where it is said that John baptized those who came to him.

John the Baptist

Out in the desert, near the River Jordan, a strange man started teaching and preaching. He was dressed in a tunic made from camel's hair and lived on honey and flying insects called locusts. People who went to see him thought he looked how the prophets must have looked in earlier times. They wondered if he was 'the promised one' or Messiah that God had said would one day save the Jewish people.

This man (who was called John) bathed or baptized people in the Jordan as a sign that their sins were washed away. John denied he was the Messiah. 'I baptize you with water but someone is coming who is much greater than I am. I'm not good enough even to undo his sandals. He will baptize you with God's Holy Spirit.'

That man was his cousin, Jesus, who also came to be baptized in the Jordan at the start of his own ministry.

The entry of Jesus into Jerusalem on the first Palm Sunday – as imagined by the sixteenth-century Italian painter Santi di Tito.

Look it Up

The Apostle Paul

After Jesus was put to death, the religious leaders in Jerusalem wanted to stop his followers from spreading his teachings. One of these leaders was a man called Saul. When journeying to a city called Damascus to hunt down any of Jesus' followers he could find there, he had a vision of Jesus. He became a follower himself and, from then on, was known as Paul.

He made three great journeys to parts of the Roman empire in what are now Turkey and Greece, spreading the news about Jesus. The early Christians who were sent out to do this are known as 'apostles'. Paul was one of the first apostles to preach the Christian faith to non-Jews.

The apostle Paul sent many letters explaining the teachings of Jesus to people he had met on his journeys.

14 † The Spread of Christianity

Once, during the three years that Jesus spent teaching, he said to one of his first disciples, Peter, 'You are a rock, and on this rock foundation I will build my church' (Matthew 16:18).

Peter became one of the leaders of the first Christians and (50 days after the resurrection) was the first to preach about Jesus in public – an event Christians remember each year at Pentecost.

During the next 70 years, Christianity reached many towns and cities around the eastern end of the Mediterranean Sea, all of which were in the Roman empire. In the following years, Christians began to take their faith to other parts of that empire: to Spain in the west, to England in the north and south to the African coast and (possibly) even to more distant places.

All this was despite the fact that the

Christianity in the Roman empire just before Constantine became emperor in the third century.

Romans frequently attacked and killed Christians. This was because Christians would not worship the Roman gods. Being a Christian at that time often meant meeting in secret and risking death when teaching about the faith. This changed in the year 312 CE, when Constantine became emperor of Rome. He became a Christian himself and later, by the end of that century, Christianity had become the official religion of the Roman empire.

In the following centuries, Christianity spread to other countries in Europe. Over the years, differences grew between the church leaders in Rome and those in Constantinople (now called Istanbul and now in Turkey).

Eventually, in 1054 CE, the Church officially split, the western half (based in Rome) becoming what we know as the Roman Catholic Church. ('Catholic' means 'universal'.) The eastern churches became known as the Orthodox Churches. ('Orthodox' means 'true' or 'correct'.)

Orthodox Churches are found especially in Greece, Russia and other eastern European countries.

Roman Catholics trace their history back to Peter, who became the first leader, or 'bishop', of the Christians in Rome. Each subsequent bishop of Rome has been known as the Pope.

The Reformation

In the centuries following this split, the Roman Catholic Church became very powerful. A number of people thought it was getting too powerful, too rich and too greedy. They also wanted the Bible to be printed in their own languages so they could learn about the faith for themselves.

A view inside of a Lutheran church in Sweden.

Two of those who wanted to reform the Church were a German called Martin Luther and a Frenchman called John Calvin. This 'reformation' resulted in arguments and wars, cruel persecution – and another split. Those who left the Roman Church to follow Luther and Calvin became known as Lutherans and Calvinists. In England, the Church was reformed but kept some of the customs of the Catholic Church and is known as the Church of England (or Anglican Church).

Members of all these reformed Churches are known as Protestants. In later years, the Protestant Churches were to divide into separate Churches such as the Baptists, Methodists and Pentecostalists.

The Church Beyond Europe

Around the time of the Reformation, Spanish explorers began to sail to Central and South America. They took their Catholic faith with them and spread Christianity among the peoples they found there. Portuguese explorers did the same in Brazil, parts of Africa, India and East Asia.

During the nineteenth century, other Christians made it their work or mission to spread Christianity in Africa and the countries of the Pacific. Meanwhile, Protestants from Europe took their faith to North America and also to Australia.

Since then, the churches in these different continents have grown rapidly. Almost half the population of Africa is now Christian. In the last 50 years, there have been increasing numbers of Protestants in Central and South America – and the Roman Catholic Church has grown throughout the United States of America. There, the Pentecostal Church and the Baptist Church have also grown rapidly.

A view inside the elaborately decorated Catholic cathedral of Santa Maria de Valencia in Spain.

Look it Up

For Christians, the Bible (especially the New Testament) is central to what they believe.

How Christians Use the Bible

Most church services include at least two readings from different parts of the Bible. In some services, one or more of the psalms (from the Book of Psalms in the Old Testament) may be read or sung.

Readings from it are also included in baptism, marriage and funeral services.

Many Christians read the Bible at home each day to learn more about God. Some gather together in groups to study the Bible together.

In Christian countries, the Bible may be part of everyday life. People may swear in court 'on the Bible' to tell the truth.

15 † The New Testament

The word 'testament' means 'promise' or 'agreement'. The word began to be used about 200 years after the time of Jesus. For Christians, the Old Testament is the promise made by God to the Jews through Abraham, Moses and the prophets. The New Testament is the promise made 'through Jesus Christ' that it is possible to have forgiveness and everlasting life .

The Old Testament is important to Christians because it was important to Jesus. It was his 'Bible'. It is also important to them because they believe it shows how God had taught his people how to live and what to believe; and also because they believe it contains many passages that look forward to the coming of Jesus.

More important to them, however, are the writings in the New Testament, and especially the Gospels.

Orthodox Christians in the Ukraine carry holy pictures showing scenes from the New Testament in a procession on the Feast of the Epiphany (see page 40).

The Gospels

The word 'gospel' means 'good news'. The Gospels were written between the years 50 CE and 130 CE. They are the only accounts of the life of Jesus, and the four writers each chose to include different details. The first and fourth Gospels are said to have been written by Matthew and John, two of Jesus' original disciples. The second (and probably first to be written down) is called St Mark's Gospel. Mark may have known Peter, who told him about Jesus.

The third Gospel is said to have been written by Luke, a Greek doctor who was probably one of the first non-Jews to become a Christian. Luke is also the author of the next book in the New Testament, the Acts of the Apostles, much of which is about the journeys of Paul.

Indian Christians meet to study the Bible.

The Epistles

Although they are printed after the Gospels in the New Testament, some of the epistles (or letters) were written earlier. The earliest are the epistles that Paul wrote to the Churches he founded during his journeys around the Mediterranean. In these letters, Paul says little about the actual life of Jesus but more about what his life, his death and resurrection and his teachings mean to those who follow Jesus.

The New Testament also contains later epistles thought to have been written by Peter, John and other apostles.

Christians understand that the books of the Bible were all written by human beings but they believe that the ideas in them were given to those writers by God – so the Bible is 'the word of God'. Some Christians believe that every word in the Bible is literally true and should be followed. Others believe they should respect its teachings but think prayerfully about what its writings mean for them today.

The Christian Bible

The Christian Bible has two parts: the Old Testament and the New Testament.

The Old Testament contains the same books that form the Jewish Bible or Tenakh (arranged in a slightly different order and with some split into two parts so there appear to be 39 books in the Old Testament). Although Jesus would have read it in its original Hebrew, it had been translated into Greek and the first Christians probably read it in Greek.

The New Testament contains 27 books:

- Four 'Gospels', which tell the story of the life, work and teachings of Jesus.
- A book called the Acts of the Apostles, which tells the story of the early preachers (or apostles) who took the Christian message to others.
- Several 'epistles' or letters, written mainly by Paul to different groups of Christians.
- A book called Revelation, which is a dream or vision about the time when Jesus comes back to earth.

It was not until the year 397 CE that Christians finally decided which books should be in their Bible – and even now there is some disagreement. Many Christians, including Roman Catholics, include a number of books about the Jews and their beliefs which are not included in the Jewish Bible. In some Bibles, they are printed as part of the Old Testament and are known as the Deuterocanon. In others, they are printed separately between the two Testaments and are called the Apocrypha.

The New Testament was first written in Greek and later translated into Latin, the language of the Roman empire. It was not until the fourteenth century that it was translated into other European languages. In more recent times, it has been translated into most of the languages of the world.

Look it Up

8 The Tenakh
13 The Man Called Jesus
14 The Spread of Christianity

The Christian faith is based on the life and teachings of Jesus.

16 ✝ 'I Believe…'

Jesus once asked his disciples, 'Who do you say that I am?' One of them, Simon Peter, answered, 'You are … the Son of the living God' (Matthew 16:16).

This is still the answer most Christians give when asked the same question. Their central belief is that God became a human being, living on earth as Jesus. They believe that not only did the Son of God live and die on earth but, three days after his death, he 'rose from the dead'.

Christians say that, in this way, Jesus showed that death is a new beginning: the start of a new life after death. They also believe that by dying on the cross, Jesus saved human beings from the results of their wrongdoings or 'sins'.

In his letters or 'epistles', Paul taught the same message: the death of Jesus on the cross showed how great God's love was for all people. Not only that, Paul said, but by rising from the dead and being taken back into heaven, Jesus had shown them that he was indeed the Son of God and that there is a new life in heaven after death.

Jesus frequently spoke about the kingdom of heaven. For Christians, it is God's dwelling place and also that of all true believers, following their life on earth. Jesus also spoke of hell as being real. In the past, the Christian Churches have taught that hell is a place where the wicked will suffer for ever. Today, most Christians place more importance on God's love and forgiveness.

The Trinity
Christians also believe that, at a festival called Pentecost, 50 days after the resurrection of Jesus, God

Body and Soul

Christians believe that each person consists of a body – and a soul living inside that body. The soul cannot be found inside the body in the way that a surgeon can find the brain. It is (they believe) both invisible and everlasting. It is what makes each person different and it lives for ever – even after the death of the body.

Some Christians say their soul is saved through faith – by their belief in Jesus.

Some say their soul will be saved by their 'works' – the good things they do during their lives on earth.

Most believe their soul is saved both by faith and by 'good works'.

The Italian painter Raphael created this painting in which he imagined the resurrection (rising to life) of Jesus happening in the setting of his own day – the sixteenth century.

The Mustard Seed

Jesus often taught his followers by telling them stories or 'parables'. He told this parable to show how his good news, or 'gospel', can spread:

A man once took a tiny mustard seed, one of the smallest seeds there is. He planted it in a field. Even though it is so very tiny, it can grow and grow until it becomes a large bush with its bright yellow flowers. Indeed, it can grow big and strong enough for birds to hide in and make their nests in its branches (Matthew 13:31–32).

Another time, to prove to his followers how strong faith can be, he told them that if they had belief in God 'no bigger than a mustard seed', then they would be able to work miracles (Matthew 17:20).

The followers of Jesus would have been familiar with the brightly flowered mustard plant which grows from a tiny seed.

A Russian holy painting, or 'icon', showing God in the three forms of the Trinity: God the Father (centre), God the Son (left) and God the Holy Spirit.

showed himself to be with the disciples in a third way. First, God had shown himself to be a loving Father. Secondly, he had lived on earth as God's Son, Jesus. At Pentecost, he came in the form of the Holy Spirit. Christians believe that God is present in the world as God the Holy Spirit.

This idea that God is known in these three ways (but is still only one Being) is called the Trinity. It does not mean that there are three Christian 'Gods' but that the one God has three forms.

As time went by, the Church tried to make sure all Christians believed the same things. So 'creeds' (summaries of belief) were written to be said when people became Christians (at baptism). Creeds are now repeated by many Christians during church services as a way of stating publicly what they believe.

Creeds

The word 'creed' comes from the Latin *credo*, which means 'I believe'.

The following creed is known as the Apostles' Creed. It was probably written in the fourth century and is divided into three sections – about God the Father, God the Son and God the Holy Spirit.

I believe in God, the Father almighty,
creator of heaven and earth.

I believe in Jesus Christ, his only Son, our Lord,
who was conceived by the Holy Spirit,
born of the Virgin Mary,
suffered under Pontius Pilate,
was crucified, died, and was buried;
he descended to the dead.
On the third day he rose again;
he ascended into heaven,
he is seated at the right hand of the Father,
and he will come to judge the living and the dead.

I believe in the Holy Spirit,
the holy catholic• Church,
the communion of saints,
the forgiveness of sins,
the resurrection of the body,
and the life everlasting. Amen.

•'catholic' here means 'universal'

Look it Up

13 The Man Called Jesus
14 The Spread of Christianity
19 Festivals and Holy Days

Christians believe they can pray anywhere but they also meet to worship together, usually in buildings called churches.

This church in India displays important Christian symbols – the cross and the bread and wine.

Church

The word 'church' has three meanings:

- the whole 'family' of all Christian believers
- a separately organized group of Christians such as the Roman Catholic Church or the Baptist Church
- a building where Christians meet for prayer and worship.

Roman Catholics, Anglicans and members of the Orthodox Churches call the main church of a particular area a 'cathedral' (literally, the *cathedra* or seat of a bishop).

Protestants sometimes use the word 'chapel' to describe their meeting place. A chapel can also be a small church or a church which is part of a school, hospital or prison.

17 ✝ In Churches, Chapels and Cathedrals

When it was against the law of the Roman empire to be Christian, Christians met in secret. It was only when the religion became legal that people began to build churches. They vary from the very old to the very new; from being richly decorated to the plain and simple. They have all been built for the worship of God.

Many churches in the West have been planned in the shape of a cross, with a spire or square tower at one end – pointing up to where people used to believe heaven was. Orthodox churches are usually planned in the shape of a square cross (like a plus sign), with a dome in the centre of the roof.

Inside Roman Catholic and Anglican churches, the main feature is the altar or holy table, used in Holy Communion services. It used to be always placed at the eastern end of the building but is now sometimes in the middle. In Orthodox churches, the altar is hidden by a screen covered with holy pictures called icons. In Protestant churches (where preaching and Bible reading is especially important), the pulpit is often in the centre of the building.

Worship

Christian worship usually takes place on a Sunday – the day of the resurrection. It usually includes praise of God by singing holy songs known as hymns, prayer (both public and private), readings from the Bible and a sermon or talk given by the priest or minister in which he or she explains part of the Bible.

In Pentecostal church services such as this one in Papua New Guinea, there is often much powerful singing, including 'Gospel music' which praises God, teaches the message of the Christian gospel and asks for social justice.

The Lord's Prayer

Jesus was once asked how people should pray. He taught them a prayer that became known as the Lord's Prayer or the 'Our Father' (from its first two words).

Our Father in heaven,
hallowed be your name,
your kingdom come, your will be done,
on earth as [it is] in heaven.
Give us today our daily bread.
Forgive us our sins
as we forgive those who sin against us.

Lead us not into temptation,
but deliver us from evil.

An ancient ending is often added to the prayer:
For the kingdom, the power
and the glory are yours
now and for ever. Amen.

The exact wording can vary. In some versions, an old word 'trespasses' is used instead of 'sins'.

Holy Communion

Worship in Orthodox, Roman Catholic and Anglican Churches usually centres on Jesus' instruction to remember him by sharing bread and wine, as he did with his disciples at the Last Supper. Such services may be called the Eucharist ('thanksgiving'), the Last Supper, Holy Communion or Mass (a title used mainly in the Roman Catholic Church). The most holy moment in these services is when the priest or minister says a prayer over the bread and wine to mark how Jesus gave his body and blood to save his people.

In Roman Catholic, Orthodox and many Anglican Churches, the priest acts as a link between God and the people (a senior priest is called a 'bishop'). Protestants do not believe that their leaders have this special role and give them titles such as 'minister' or 'pastor' – the latter word meaning 'shepherd'.

Christians believe God hears every prayer.

Private Prayer

Many Christians try to remember to say daily prayers, either in a room where they can be alone or wherever is convenient. Some families pray together before a meal.

For Christians, prayer is not just a matter of asking for things. Prayer means:

- praising God for his greatness
- thanking him for his gifts such as food, health and other blessings
- saying sorry for having done wrong things
- asking for his help for relatives, those who are ill or suffering and others in need
- asking for help for themselves.

For their private prayers, some Christians use books of printed prayers. Many simply talk to God in their own words as they would to a friend.

Look it Up

13 The Man Called Jesus
14 The Spread of Christianity
18 The Christian Life
10 What Does it Mean
to Be Jewish? (Amen)

Christians try to live their lives by following Jesus' commandments to love God and to love one another.

Giving to Charity

All Christians are expected to give money to help run their own church and to both Christian and non-Christian charities. In the past, Christians have given large sums of money to build churches, hospitals and schools.

Many Christian organizations and charities (such as Christian Aid) help those in poorer countries. They send clothes and tins of food abroad when disasters such as earthquakes or flooding occur. They also help people in Third World countries to fight disease and hunger themselves by providing tools, machinery and money, and by teaching new skills to local people. They also try to persuade politicians to see that wealth is more fairly spread between rich and poor countries.

Look it Up

18 ✝ The Christian Life

Jesus was once asked which was the most important of the Ten Commandments (given originally to Moses). His answer was to give a summary of all ten:

' "Love the Lord your God with all your heart, and with all your soul, and with all your mind." This is the greatest and the most important commandment. The second most important commandment is like it: "Love your neighbour as you love yourself" ' (Matthew 22:37–39).

Besides following the commandment to 'love your neighbour', Christians also remember Jesus' words in the book of Matthew about the hungry, the homeless and those who are ill: 'Anything you do for one of those, however humble, you do for me.'

For most Christians, this means helping those around them, giving money to good causes and working to make the world a better place.

Helping the Neighbours

Many Christians try to do this in their daily lives, perhaps by gardening or shopping for someone who is housebound or old. They may take someone who cannot drive to a meeting, to hospital or simply for an outing. They may visit friends or neighbours who are in hospital.

Some Christians become prison visitors or do voluntary work for complete strangers. Many churches organize clubs and meetings for the elderly and lonely, and Christian organizations like the Salvation Army provide special help for the hungry and homeless.

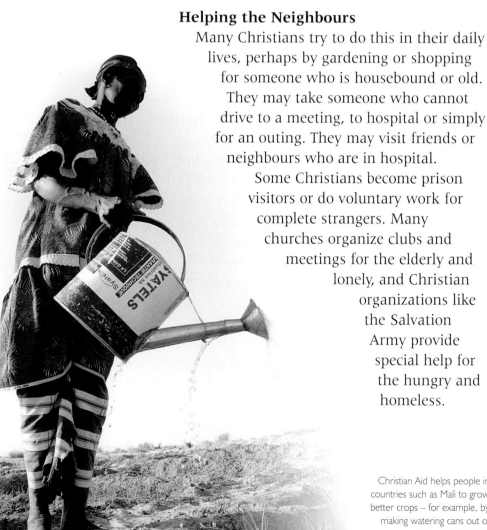

Christian Aid helps people in countries such as Mali to grow better crops – for example, by making watering cans out of recycled materials.

Christians mark important stages of their lives in special ways. Many believe the most important is when they become a Christian and a member of the worldwide Church.

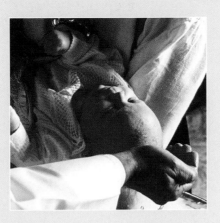

Baptism

The service of baptism is both a 'joining' and a naming ceremony because, if the person being baptized (or christened) is a baby, that is when he or she is given their first (or Christian) name.

The Roman Catholic and some Protestant Churches usually baptize children when they are babies. In the Russian Orthodox Church, babies are baptized when they are eight days old. A person can, of course, join the Church through baptism when they are older if they were not baptized as a child. At these and at infant baptism services, prayers are said and a little water is sprinkled on the person's forehead in the sign of a cross.

Baptists (and some other Protestant Christians) only baptize people when they are old enough to understand what it means. Instead of sprinkling a little water on their forehead, the person being baptized is immersed in a bath of water for a few seconds – just as Jesus was immersed by John in the River Jordan. In some Orthodox Churches, infants are baptized by total immersion.

In Roman Catholic and Anglican Churches, there is another service called confirmation, when people who were baptized as babies take upon themselves the responsibilities of being adult members of their church.

Marriage

Christians believe that, ideally, a man and woman should marry for life or 'till death us do part'. Only after the death of one partner is remarriage possible. This is based on Jesus' teaching that remarriage after divorce is wrong. Even so, some Christians allow the remarriage of divorced couples in church.

Death

During his life on earth, Jesus often spoke about death. Sometimes he told his followers that death is not the end of life; for example, he once said, 'Whoever … believes in me shall never die' – meaning they shall have everlasting life in heaven.

Because of this, Christians believe that death is not an ending but the beginning of a future life without end. Because of a belief that the actual body would rise up and live again, some Christians have been very much against cremation. Most Christians now believe that only the soul has 'life everlasting' so they no longer object to cremation.

Pilgrimage

Some Christians make special journeys to holy places such as Jerusalem to show their love for God. Such journeys are called pilgrimages. Other places of Christian pilgrimage include Lourdes in France, where Christians believe Mary the mother of Jesus has been seen by believers; Santiago de Compostela in Spain, where James (one of Jesus' disciples) is said to have been buried – and Rome, the centre of the Roman Catholic Church.

Pilgrims who have made the journey to Rome gather there in St Peter's Square.

Most Christian festivals mark events in the life of Jesus.

Advent

Many Christians call the four weeks before Christmas 'Advent'. The name Advent comes from a Latin word meaning 'coming' or 'arrival' – so Advent is a time of preparation for the celebration of Jesus' birth at Christmas. Christians traditionally use this time to think about what is wrong with their lives and how they can do better. It is also when they remember Jesus' promise that he will come to earth a second time.

Some Christians use special Advent calendars to mark the days leading up to Christmas, or make Advent wreaths in which are placed four candles to mark the Sundays of Advent. In the centre is a larger white candle (lit on Christmas Day) representing 'Jesus the light of the world'.

19 † Festivals and Holy Days

For the early Christians, every Sunday was a festival. Each week, it was a celebration of the resurrection of Jesus. After some years, Christians began to make a special, yearly observance of this event at Easter. Christmas was not celebrated until several centuries later.

The festivals marking events in the life of Jesus are celebrated in the half of the year leading from Christmas through to early summer. In the second half of the year, Christians think more about his teachings.

Christmas

At Christmas, Christians celebrate the day Jesus was born in Bethlehem. For them, this is not just a birthday but a celebration of the incarnation, the coming of God into the world in the person of Jesus. As Jesus is sometimes called 'the light of the world', the Church decided to celebrate his birthday at the time of pagan and Roman mid-winter festivals (25 December). Orthodox Christians celebrate Christmas on 6/7 January.

Twelve days after Christmas comes the festival of Epiphany, which recalls the visit of wise men from a foreign country to the baby Jesus. Sometimes called the three kings (because they appeared to be important people), they represent the first non-Jews to honour Jesus.

A group of children prepare to act out the story of the first Christmas.

Holy Week and Eastertide

The 40 days leading up to Easter are known to Christians as Lent, when they remember the 40 days Jesus spent fasting in the wilderness in preparation for his three-year ministry of teaching and healing. Christians spend Lent thinking about their wrongdoings and how they can do better in the future, and preparing for Easter. At one time, they fasted quite strictly during Lent.

The week before Easter is called Holy Week. It begins with Palm Sunday when Christians remember how Jesus entered Jerusalem, seated on a donkey. Cheering crowds tore down palm branches from nearby trees to wave in celebration. Nowadays, when Christians go to church on this day, they may receive small crosses made out of folded strips of palm. These are reminders of the joy of the first Palm Sunday and also of Jesus' death by crucifixion five days later.

The Thursday night before his crucifixion, Jesus had a 'Last Supper' with his disciples, which was probably a Passover meal. Christians believe it was the start of a new 'covenant', or agreement, which promises forgiveness to all who believe. Christians remember this at Holy Communion.

A palm leaf cross.

Then comes Good Friday, a day of mourning when Christians recall the three hours Jesus spent nailed to a cross before he died. In many churches, the main service on Good Friday takes place between midday and 3pm (the hours Jesus is said to have hung on the cross). In some towns there are re-enactments of the crucifixion.

For most Christians, the main festival of the year comes on the Sunday after Good Friday. On this day, Easter Sunday, they celebrate their belief that Jesus triumphed over death.

A nineteenth-century painting of the Last Supper showing Jesus sharing bread and wine with his disciples.

Ascension and Pentecost

During the days following Easter, Jesus appeared several times to his followers. Then, 40 days after Easter, he led his friends to the top of a hill outside Jerusalem. There, a low cloud covered the hilltop and hid him from them. When the cloud lifted, he was gone, as the Acts of the Apostles in the New Testament describes.

This event is called the ascension and is remembered as Ascension Day.

Ten days later, his followers met in an upstairs room in Jerusalem. As they prayed, they heard a sound like 'the rush of a mighty wind'. They saw what looked like tongues of fire on their heads but were unharmed. They accepted this as a sign that the Holy Spirit had come to each of them (and to all who believe).

In most countries, this festival is called Pentecost, because it occurs 50 days after Easter, *pente* being Greek for 50. Another English name is Whitsun (originally 'White Sunday', a day when Christians were baptized – for which event they wore white clothes).

Look it Up

Christians believe they should show their faith by the way they live their lives.

Saint Francis gave up all his wealth and dedicated his life to helping the poor. He was also famous for his gentleness towards all creatures, who trusted him and seemed to listen to him.

Saints of the Church

Some Christians have become known as 'saints'. The word 'saint' comes from a Latin word *sanctus,* meaning 'holy'.

Christians believe that saints are believers who have been given strength or 'grace' to do some special work for God. That gift might be being a great teacher or healer, being very brave or patient, or feeling able to give up their whole life to prayer.

The early apostles are often called saints (such as Saint Peter or Saint Paul). There are many other saints, such as Saint Nicholas (who became known to some people as Santa Claus) and Saint Francis of Assisi.

The word 'saint' is also sometimes used to mean any faithful believer.

20 † Christianity in Action

Near the end of his life on earth, Jesus told his disciples that they would 'receive power and will tell people about me everywhere'. Christians believe the disciples received that power at the first Pentecost. Ever since, they have believed all Christians have a duty to spread the gospel in different countries around the world.

Even so, there have sometimes been disagreements between different groups of Christians, some being serious enough to split the Church in two (as happened when it divided into separate Catholic and Orthodox Churches). Occasionally there have even been wars between Christians – for example, when Catholics have fought Protestants. During the last 50 years, the various Churches have begun to work and worship together more than they did in the past.

The Growth of the Church

More than one third of the world's population now describe themselves as Christian. The faith is still growing, especially in Central and South America and Africa. Since the end of Communism in Russia, numbers have grown there. More people are becoming Christian in China and Indonesia. In Europe, it is a different story. The numbers actually going to church each Sunday have got much smaller in recent years.

In the United States of America, the various Protestant Churches (including Pentecostal ones) have become increasingly strong. In the year 2000, it was estimated that 44 per cent of the population went to church on Sundays.

Chinese Roman Catholic Christians hold a procession as a reminder of how Jesus had to carry his cross to the place where he was crucified.

The Guatemalan Street

Pepe and Julio were street boys. Once they were lucky. They found a blue plastic sheet. By tearing it in half, they each had something to sleep under. Even though the days are warm, the nights can be very cold in Guatemala. Julio also found a cardboard box. By squashing it flat, he made a mattress.

Like many other homeless boys, Julio lived at El Hoyo, which means 'the hole'. It was a piece of wasteland near the bus station. If he was lucky, he'd find some half-eaten food (such as a chicken leg) that had been thrown away by a passenger.

It has been calculated that 40 million children live on the streets of the cities in Central and South America. Some are there because their families have no money to look after them. Others have lost their parents because of civil war, drought, hurricanes, the AIDS epidemic or city violence.

They become victims of harassment and violent abuse. Some are shot. Many seek to numb the pain and loneliness of life on the streets by turning to solvent abuse. They have a life expectancy of around four years on the street.

A charity called Toybox, set up by Christians, helps these street children by building 'safe' houses in which they can live and by providing food and training for proper jobs. Toybox is working for a world where there will be no street children.

Faith in Action

Over the last 200 years, Christians in wealthy 'Western' countries have learned more about the poverty, famines and injustices that create misery, suffering and death in poorer countries. They also now understand that many people suffer simply because of the colour of their skin: they are victims of racism.

Many Christians know that if they are to live their lives following the example of Jesus, then they must bring food and water, medicine and justice to those in need – just as Jesus cared for the people he met. Christians have fought to end slavery and to improve prison conditions – but know there is still work to be done.

Look it Up

For Muslims, the Prophet Muhammad is the last and greatest of the prophets of God.

Islam

The teaching that the Prophet Muhammad shared with his people is known as Islam. Islam means 'peace' or 'acceptance' of God's will. Its followers are called Muslims. In Arabic, the word for God is *Allah*.

The Prophet did not believe he was creating a new religion. He was reminding his followers of the message once taught by earlier prophets such as Ibrahim (also known as Abraham), Musa (Moses) and Isa (Jesus): that there is one and only one true God. This teaching is called *tawhid*.

The Prophet Muhammad is greatly honoured by Muslims. He is never shown in a picture and if Muslims say his name, they follow it with the words 'Peace be upon him'. In Arabic, that is written:

Look it Up

21 ☾ The Prophet

The Prophet Muhammad lived in what is now Saudi Arabia from about 570 to 632 CE. Muslims believe he received his 'call' and the revelation of the Qur'an from the angel Gabriel (or Jibril, as he is known in Arabic) in the year 610 CE.

At that time, there was much fighting between local tribes, and the poor were ill-treated by the rich.

The Call of the Prophet

Muhammad's parents died when he was six and he was looked after by his grandfather and later by an uncle in the city of Makkah. Muhammad wasn't taught to read or write but, by the time he was 20, he was working for his uncle, who was a trader in that city. Because Muhammad never tried to swindle customers by overcharging them or by cheating on the weight of something, he became known as *al-Amin*, which means 'the Trustworthy'.

One morning, his uncle told him that a wealthy widow called Khadijah (who also lived in Makkah) was looking for a reliable young man to travel with, and care for, her camels which she sent to other cities, carrying goods she was buying and selling.

Muhammad went to her house and was offered the job. He worked hard and honestly, and Khadijah's business prospered. She eventually sent him a proposal of marriage. The wedding took place and it proved to be a long and happy marriage.

Muslim traders used to travel in groups called 'caravans' for safety – for example, when carrying silk from the east to Arab countries and Europe along what was known as the Silk Road.

Although Muhammad knew he was fortunate, there were times he wanted to feel close to God, so he would walk out of the city of Makkah, north to a hill called Mount Hira, and especially to one particular cave, high up in the mountain. There he could be alone to think.

One particular night, when Muhammad was in the cave, he heard a voice. In front of him he saw an angel.

'Recite,' said the angel.

'What should I recite?' asked Muhammad.

This happened three times and then the angel spoke again: 'Recite, in the name of God.'

Muhammad repeated the words the angel then spoke to him until he knew them by heart. Suddenly, the angel was gone and Muhammad was alone.

Months passed. Many times Muhammad went back to the cave and saw nothing. Ten months later, the angel appeared to him again, saying, 'Warn the people. Tell them they must worship and praise God and give up their wicked ways and wrongdoing.'

After that, the angel Jibril (or Gabriel) appeared often to Muhammad, giving him many more messages which he was to repeat to those who would listen to what he had to say. Muhammad taught them the message of the angel: that there is only one God.

All that the angel told Muhammad was later written down in a book, known as the Qur'an. It is treasured by all Muslims as the word of God.

A mother teaches her daughter the Muslim faith.

Maulid al-Nabi

The Prophet is said to have been born on the twelfth day of the Islamic month called Rabi ul-Awwal in the year 570 CE and to have died at the same time of the year in 632 CE.

The festival of Maulid al-Nabi marks these two events. Although some Muslims do not mark this 'Day of the Prophet' because there is no basis in the Qur'an for doing so, it is a popular time of celebration in many communities. Those Muslims who observe it do so by telling the story of the Prophet to their children.

Pilgrims climb Mount Hira, in which is the cave where the Qur'an was revealed to the Prophet Muhammad.

Following the death of the Prophet Muhammad, Islam spread rapidly both east and westwards.

Al Hijrah

After the Prophet had received the first revelations from the angel Jibril, he shared them with the people of Makkah. Many accepted the teaching: 'There is no god but God.'

Others (who worshipped idols and other gods) thought that if the Prophet persuaded everyone to destroy their idols, nobody would visit the city and they would become poor. They wanted to kill the Prophet.

Muslims believe that God warned the Prophet in a dream of the danger. With his friend and servant, Abu Bakr, the Prophet escaped. They made the difficult journey across the desert to the city of Yathrib (later named Madinah) where the Prophet could preach in safety.

Eight years later, in the year 630 CE, the Prophet returned in triumph to Makkah.

The departure, or 'al Hijrah', of the Prophet from Makkah is celebrated annually as the first day of the Muslim year.

22 ☾ The Spread of Islam

Following the death of the Prophet Muhammad, there was disagreement about who should be the next leader. The choice was between Ali, who had been married to the Prophet's daughter, and Muhammad's friend Abu Bakr.

The Four Khalifahs

Abu Bakr was chosen and became the first *khalifah* or leader. Two years later, he died and a man called Umar ibn al-Khattab became *khalifah*. When he was murdered in 644 CE, his place was taken by Uthman – who was also killed. Twelve years later, Ali (the Prophet's son-in-law) finally became the fourth *khalifah*. The word *khalifah* is sometimes written as 'caliph'.

During the lifetime of the Prophet, most of what is now Saudi Arabia became Muslim. Within 100 years of his death, Islam had spread further afield. First, its armies had marched into nearby countries and then moved further on, conquering as they went. The armies were quickly followed by traders and teachers. By 732 CE, Muslims ruled from Spain to India, including southern France, all of northern Africa, Egypt, Arabia and what are now Iraq and Iran.

Masjid al-Nabi (the Mosque of the Prophet) at Madinah in what is now Saudi Arabia. The green dome is said to mark the burial place of the Prophet.

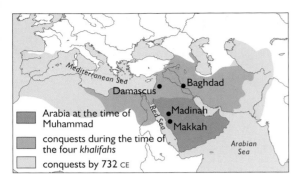

Arabia at the time of Muhammad

conquests during the time of the four *khalifahs*

conquests by 732 CE

The early spread of Islam.

Look it Up

21 The Prophet
26 Living a Muslim Life (Al Hajj)
28 Conflicts and Convictions
37 Hinduism in India –
and Around the World
58 Faith Around the World Today
59 Religious Conflict

Emperor Suleiman the Magnificent.

The Muslim Empires

In the following centuries, the Muslim world grew stronger and richer. Several Islamic empires were established, including the mighty Ottoman empire, which lasted from about 1300 to 1920 CE. Centred on what is now Turkey, at one time it stretched from Algeria in North Africa east to Basra in Iraq, and northwards to include Hungary and parts of Russia. Its greatest ruler was Emperor Suleiman in the sixteenth century. His palaces in his capital Istanbul so dazzled Western visitors that they called him Suleiman the Magnificent.

At about the same time, another Muslim empire, the Mughal empire, came into being when a Muslim prince, Babur, invaded India.

After defeating the Indian army, he celebrated his victory by building a garden and forbade the killing of cows because that offended the local Hindu population. Babur made peace with the Hindu kingdoms of southern India and encouraged the building of Hindu temples.

Under a later ruler, Akbar, the Mughal empire stretched across India.

The Decline of the Muslim World

In the year 1258 CE, tribes from the north known as Mongols reached the city of Baghdad in what is now Iraq. They attacked, killed thousands and destroyed the city and its libraries.

In the year 1492, Europeans won control of Spain from the Muslims. These two events helped to decrease the power of Islam. Later, from about 1700 CE to 1950, large parts of the Muslim world came under Western rule. The Mughal empire was gradually conquered by the British as they took control of India. In 1857, for example, what had been the great Muslim city of Delhi was captured by the British, ending 1,000 years of Muslim rule.

Many Muslim countries were now ruled as colonies by the British, the French and the Dutch. In Tunisia, the French created laws that made traditional Muslim medicine against the law. In some places, Islamic libraries were destroyed and treasures taken back to Western cities.

The Qur'an says heaven is like a perfect garden. The garden of the Alhambra Palace at Granada in southern Spain tries to reflect this.

Muslims regard their holy book as God's own word, revealed to the Prophet and not written by human beings.

A surah or chapter heading from a fourteenth-century copy of the Qur'an from the Mamluk empire based on Egypt.

The Language of the Qur'an

The Qur'an is written in a historic or traditional form of Arabic. Many Muslims do not speak or understand Arabic and even those who speak modern Arabic may not understand the language of the Qur'an. It is sometimes translated into modern languages but Muslims believe that no translation can say exactly what the original means.

Young Muslims often go to Qur'an School to learn sections by heart – in its traditional language. The book itself is treated with great respect. Muslims always wash before touching it and never touch it while eating or drinking. Nor must it ever touch the ground.

Because Arabic letters are very different from Western ones, different English spellings are sometimes used to imitate the sound of an Arabic word – which is why the word 'Qur'an' is sometimes spelled 'Koran' in English.

23 ☾ The Qur'an

The holy book of Islam is the Qur'an: the collection of sayings and messages believed to have been brought by the angel Jibril from God to the Prophet Muhammad. Muslims believe it is God's final and complete teaching for his people. It is neither a history book nor a book of stories but a collection of teachings, laws and wise sayings.

The Revelation

Muslims believe that the Prophet Muhammad could neither read nor write. On each occasion that the angel Jibril brought more of God's teachings to him on Mount Hira, the Prophet learned them by heart. When he returned to Makkah, he repeated them to friends, who also learned them by heart.

After the Prophet had moved to Madinah, the angel Jibril revealed more teachings to him. It is said that the complete revelation took place over a period of 23 years.

After the Prophet's death, his friend Abu Bakr wanted to keep all the teachings safe. A man called Zaid ibn Thabit collected the sayings together and wrote them down just as the Prophet had dictated them. He made no changes. Since that day, they have been written or printed in exactly the same words.

They are known as the Qur'an because the word *qur'an* is Arabic for 'recitation' and the angel's first word to the Prophet was 'recite'.

The Surahs

The Qur'an contains 114 'chapters' called 'surahs', sometimes written 'suras'. These are always arranged in the same order. It is said that the angel Jibril ordered that they should be arranged this way.

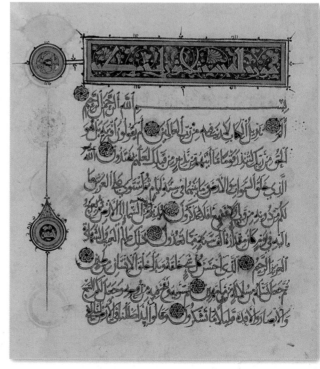

A decorated surah in a seventeenth-century Chinese copy of the Qur'an.

• After *al-Fatihah* (see right) come the longer surahs, revealed to the Prophet in Madinah after the first Muslim state had been created. Because of this, they include laws by which countries should be governed, instructions to judges to be merciful and also instructions about daily life. For example, Muslims should dress modestly and not be greedy. There are other rules forbidding Muslims to charge or pay interest on money that they lend or borrow.

• Then come the shorter surahs, mostly revealed while the Prophet was still living in Makkah. These teach Muslims about God, about creation, life after death and the greatness of God.

Each surah (except surah 9) begins with the words, 'In the name of God, the compassionate, the merciful.' These words are called the 'Bismillah'. Muslims say the Bismillah before eating or doing any important job as a way of asking God's blessing. It is said that the Bismillah was written on Jibril's wings.

The Sunnah

Muslims try to live their lives not only by the Qur'an but also by the 'Sunnah'. The word means 'method' or 'example'. The Sunnah is a collection of wisdom which contains a record of all that the Prophet Muhammad did and also the 'Hadith', a collection of his sayings.

Look it Up

21 The Prophet
22 The Spread of Islam
24 The Five Pillars

Al-Fatihah

As part of their daily prayers, Muslims repeat the opening words of the Qur'an, known as *al-Fatihah* or *Umm al-Kitab* ('mother of the book'):

In the name of God,
The most Gracious,
The most Merciful,
All praise be to God alone, the Lord of Creation,
The most Gracious, the most Merciful
King of Judgment Day!
You alone we worship and to you alone we pray for help.
Guide us in the right way – the way of those you have blessed, not the way of those that have been condemned by you or of those who go astray.

Surah 1

Young Muslims study their holy book at Qur'an School in Malaysia.

Islam has five 'pillars' or rules which Muslims should follow in order to live a good life.

The Five Pillars

1 *Shahadah*: the statement of faith
2 *Salah* or *salat*: prayer
3 *Zakat* or *zakah*: helping the needy
4 *Sawm* (sometimes written *saum*): fasting in the month of Ramadan
5 *Hajj*: pilgrimage to Makkah

An engraving of the Shahadah in the Taynal mosque in Tripoli, Lebanon.

A decorated Muslim prayer mat.

24 ☾ The Five Pillars

The Muslim religion lays down five duties for its followers. By observing these five duties or 'pillars', Muslims believe they are obeying God's will. They are called pillars because Muslims feel they support them in their lives in the same way that pillars support a building. They are mentioned throughout the Qur'an.

The Shahadah

Muslims learn that the first duty of Islam is to make a statement of their faith. This is done by saying words known as the 'Shahadah': 'There is no god but God and Muhammad is his Prophet.'

In Arabic it is:
La ila' ha illallah Muhammad ur rasulullah.

It is by saying the Shahadah (and believing it) that a person becomes a Muslim.

Salah

'Salah' means 'prayer'. The Muslim holy book, the Qur'an, repeatedly says how important it is to pray – and to pray at set times: 'Prayer at fixed times has been enjoined on the believers.'

Because of this, Muslims pray five times a day, at times the Prophet told them to do. These times are:

- between the first sign of daylight and sunrise
- just after midday
- in the middle of the afternoon
- after sunset but before dark
- when it is dark.

Muslims may say these prayers in any place that is clean – provided they are themselves clean. The special act of washing before prayer is called *wudu*.

To pray, Muslims face in the direction of Makkah. When they are ready, they usually put down a special prayer mat before they say their set prayers in Arabic.

A Muslim shows he accepts God's will during his act of 'salah'.

A different position is taken for each part of the prayer.

First, those praying stand to pay attention to God, then they bow to show respect to God. This is followed by two prostrations (low bows touching the ground with forehead, knees, nose and palms) to show submission to the will of God. Between each of these prostrations, those praying sit back on their heels. Special words are said at each point, and all the movements (or *rak'ah*) are repeated two, three or four times according to the time of day.

Muslims also say their own private prayers in their own language.

Zakat

'Zakat' (or 'zakah') means 'that which makes pure'. It is the duty or obligation of all those who can afford it to give money or food to the poor and others in need – for example those who have suffered from a disaster such as an earthquake. It may also be given to help with the building of a hospital or mosque or to help a student to study at a college or university.

Zakah is not something a Muslim chooses to do because he or she feels kind or generous. Nor is it a tax paid to a government. It is a duty to God. Islam teaches that paying zakah is good for the person receiving but also for the giver: 'Those that pay zakah will be rewarded by God and will have nothing to fear.'

In many places, the collection and giving of zakah is organized by the local mosque. Zakah is usually paid each year at the festival of Id-ul-Fitr and is paid by women and children as well as men – before attending morning prayers.

Distributing 'zakah' outside a mosque in Karachi, Pakistan.

Helping Others

Besides paying zakah, Muslims are taught that it is good to help others in need. This story is told about Umar, the second of the *khalifahs* (and therefore the ruler at that time of all Muslims).

Umar once visited a place near Madinah. There, he saw a woman heating a pan of water on an open fire. Around her, her children were crying. Umar asked what was wrong.

Not knowing who he was, the woman said, 'We can't afford anything to eat. I'm heating water in the hope it will keep my children quiet.'

Umar went into Madinah, took flour and butter and other food from the city's storerooms, and brought them back to the woman. He relit the fire, cooked a meal and fed the children himself. When they had eaten, the woman (still not knowing who he was) turned to Umar. 'May God bless you. You should be the ruler of all Muslims.'

Look it Up

Hajj: 26 Living a Muslim Life
Sawm: 27 Fasting and Festivals
See also: 22 The Spread of Islam
(The Four Khalifahs)

The place where Muslims gather together to worship God is called a mosque.

25 ☾ Mosque

The Imam

At Friday prayers, there may be a sermon or talk. This is usually given by the 'imam', a leader or teacher chosen by the other Muslims at that mosque because of his wisdom and knowledge of the Qur'an. The imam or other preacher may stand by the mihrab, sometimes on stone steps, to give his sermon.

Although Muslims can worship anywhere that is clean, the Qur'an says that whenever 40 men live in the same area, there should be a mosque in that place. Many mosques are large handsome buildings, often with a huge dome. In other places, especially where there are fewer Muslims, an ordinary house may have been converted into a mosque.

Going to Mosque

Many mosques have a tall tower called a minaret. Five times a day, at the set times, a man called the *mu'adhin* (sometimes spelled 'muezzin') traditionally calls Muslims from the minaret to pray to God. The prayer call is known as the *adhan* (or 'azan').

The most important prayers of the week are those said after noon on a Friday. At this time, many Muslim men go to the mosque to pray together and to worship God. Women may go to mosque but most pray at home at this time.

At the entrance to each mosque, there is a place for worshippers to take off their shoes and leave them, making sure the dirty soles of the shoes are not left pointing upwards towards God. Worshippers then go to a special room to wash so that they are clean when they pray to God.

An imam teaches worshippers inside a mosque in Sudan.

Look it Up

Inside a Mosque

There are no chairs or seats in the main prayer hall. Often there are mats on which Muslims can kneel and prostrate themselves to pray. (In Arabic, the word for 'mosque' is *masjid*: 'a place of prostration'.)

Because Muslims are taught always to face Makkah when praying, there is (in every mosque) an empty arch (called a 'mihrab') on one wall, which shows the direction (or 'qiblah') of Makkah.

The 'mihrab' shows worshippers the direction of Makkah, the direction in which they should face when praying.

There are never any pictures or statues of humans or animals in a mosque. This is because the Prophet thought people might worship them instead of God. But there are often many beautiful carpets or hangings, decorated with patterns or words from the Qur'an. There is never any music during Islamic worship, which is based on the word of God, as written in the Qur'an.

Besides the main area (called the Prayer Hall or Room), there may be a separate area where women can pray. There may also be a courtyard and rooms used for teaching and meetings.

The National Mosque of Malaysia in the city of Kuala Lumpur.

Ilm

Muslim scientists invented many scientific tools such as test tubes and flasks. They worked out the rules of optics (the way light works). They created the first hospitals and surgical tools. They developed the manufacture of paper and taught people how to find their way using a compass.

They studied the stars and worked out the precise length of a year. They also developed the science of mathematics (including geometry and algebra), creating the ways we still do sums. They invented the number 0 or zero. Indeed all the numerals used throughout the West (1,2,3 etc) are called Arabic numerals.

Muslims created the first ever university in Cairo in Egypt in 970 CE and also the first public libraries.

All this happened, it is said, because the Prophet Muhammad stated that it was the duty of every Muslim, male or female, to seek knowledge. This pursuit to learn new things and to develop new inventions is known as *ilm*. It was the main driving force of Muslim society in the period from roughly 500 CE to 1100 when there was less scholarship and study in Europe.

In more recent centuries, some Muslim teachers have narrowed the idea of *ilm* to religious knowledge.

The Emam mosque in Isfahan, Iran.

**Islam shows Muslims
how to live each
stage of life.**

Whispering the Shahadah into a newborn
baby's ear.

The 'city' of tents at Mina where pilgrims stay
on the final stage of the Hajj (see opposite).

Look it Up

26 ☾ Living a Muslim Life

For Muslims, family life is very important. Muslim parents have a duty to see their children grow up understanding the faith. As soon as a baby is born, its father whispers the Shahadah into its ear. By hearing these words the baby is welcomed into the faith.

Growing Up Muslim

Muslim children learn about their religion by watching their parents and seeing how they pray five times a day. As they get older, they are expected to work hard at school and to help with the housework. Going out to parties alone is discouraged – especially for girls. All teenagers are expected to show respect to older people because they know more about life than the young do.

Muslims often live in large family groups and members of the whole family help each other at all times.

Marriage

The Qur'an encourages all Muslims to marry and to have children. It also says that a man should have no more than four wives. In Western countries, it is against the law for a Muslim to have more than one wife. In those countries where it is not against the law, very few Muslim men now do this – though some marry a second wife if the first is unable to have children or if she becomes too ill to look after the children.

For Muslims, a marriage is not only the joining of two people but also the joining of two families. For this reason, the choice of partner is seen as a matter of importance to the whole family and so marriages are often 'arranged' by parents and older relatives who, it is said, can best see who would be suitable for their child.

Even where weddings are 'arranged', the young people have the right to refuse the chosen partner. Islamic law forbids forced marriages. Divorce is discouraged but is not forbidden if the marriage has completely failed.

Death

Muslims try to see that nobody dies alone. When someone is dying, the family and friends gather round and ask the dying person for forgiveness for any harm they have done. If possible, the dying person is reminded of the Shahadah – so the person dies as a believer. Burial takes place on the day of death or as near to it as possible. Muslims are never cremated but buried with their heads turned to face Makkah.

Al Hajj

The fifth pillar of Islam is to make a once-in-a-lifetime pilgrimage or journey to Makkah. The word for this duty is 'hajj' (which means 'effort' or 'purpose').

Over 2 million pilgrims make the Hajj each year. As they approach Makkah, they put on pilgrim dress. For a man, this is two pieces of white unsewn cloth. Women cover their whole bodies except their hands and faces. The purpose of this clothing is to stress equality: nobody should look more important than anyone else.

When they enter the courtyard of the Great Mosque, the pilgrims walk barefoot seven times round the 'Ka'bah'. This is a granite building in the shape of a cube; twelve metres long, ten metres wide and fifteen metres high. (The word *ka'bah* means 'cube'.) Muslims believe the first Ka'bah was built by the first man, Adam. Later, a new Ka'bah was built by Ibrahim (or Abraham). It was kept holy for many years – but was then used for pagan worship until the Prophet Muhammad yet again made it a place for worship to the one God.

When Muslims make the Hajj, they believe they are following not only in the footsteps of the Prophet but also in those of Adam and of Ibrahim.

The Ka'bah is covered in a black silk and cotton cloth with the words of the Qur'an embroidered upon it. Inside, the Ka'bah is unfurnished except for gold and silver lamps. Ordinary pilgrims do not enter. From the Ka'bah pilgrims walk or run seven times between the two small hills of Safa and Marwah, which are within Makkah. Between them is a spring (called Zamzam) and pilgrims take water from it home to those too ill to make the Hajj.

The most important part of the Hajj is when pilgrims travel to the nearby Plain of Arafat and stand and pray in the heat from noon till sunset, asking God for forgiveness. Finally they go to a place called Mina near Makkah and throw stones at three pillars to show they reject evil. An animal is sacrificed in memory of how Ibrahim was ready to sacrifice his own son for God. Male pilgrims have their heads shaved.

The Hajj ends with the festival of Id-ul-Adha.

This diagram shows the stages of the Hajj.

The centre of Makkah during the Hajj, showing the Ka'bah in the centre of the courtyard of the Great Mosque.

Ramadan is the most important month in the Muslim calendar.

The Islamic Calendar

The Islamic calendar is based on the movements of the moon. Each of its twelve months is only 29 or 30 days long (the time between one new moon and the next). This means that Muslim years are usually eleven days shorter than Western years and therefore Muslim festivals move forwards through the Western calendar. For example, the month of Ramadan happens a little earlier in each Western year.

Islamic years are dated from 'al Hijrah', which occurred in 622 CE, and are numbered AH.

An Arabic calendar for the Western month of August 2006 CE with the Western dates in black (reading from right to left, each 'week' begins on a Saturday). The dates in red show the matching dates in the Muslim months of Rajab and Sha'ban in the year 1427 AH.

Look it Up

27 ☾ Fasting and Festivals

Muslims are required to celebrate just two festivals: Id-ul-Fitr and Id-ul-Adha. *Id* (sometimes spelled *Eid* and pronounced 'eed') means 'celebration'. Many Muslims also celebrate other special days in each year – and observe the holy month of Ramadan.

Ramadan

Ramadan is a special month of the Muslim year because it was the month in which the Prophet began to receive the teaching of Islam from the angel Jibril (or Gabriel). To remind themselves of this, Muslims fast each of the 30 days of Ramadan during daylight hours. They also fast as a way of showing to themselves that their mind is stronger than their body.

During their fast, Muslims neither eat, drink nor smoke from dawn until it is dark again at night. *Sawm* (fasting) is one of the five rules or 'pillars' of Islam.

All adult Muslims are expected to fast but very old people, those who are ill or on a long journey and women who are pregnant or feeding a baby are excused. So too are young children but most try to fast once they reach the age of twelve. Some younger ones will fast for part of the day. During Ramadan, Muslims are also meant to say extra prayers and to try to read the whole of the Qur'an.

Before sunrise, Muslims have a filling meal called *suhoor,* when they eat bread with olive oil, rice or porridge, boiled eggs or dates and other fruit. After sunset, they end that day's fast with a snack (*iftar*), which might consist of a few dates or nuts, savoury pastries and fruit drinks. After evening prayers, they share in the main family meal of the day.

Id-ul-Fitr

The first day of Shawwal (the month following Ramadan) is called Id-ul-Fitr – 'the feast of fast-breaking'. It is a time to rejoice at having successfully faced the challenge of fasting.

Early morning prayers may take place out of doors so that there is room for all those who want to take part. Everyone wears their best new clothes. Next, the men may go to a cemetery to say a prayer beside the family grave. Then it is time for families to visit relatives and friends to swap presents and to give each other sweets, sugared almonds and nuts. In the Middle East, a favourite food is baklava. These are little cakes or sweets made from filo pastry filled with chopped nuts and soaked in honey.

Muslims wish each other *Id Mubarak* ('Blessed be your celebration') and exchange Id cards. Id-ul-Fitr is sometimes called Little or Lesser Id. Although it may last three days, it is shorter than 'Big Id' – Id-ul-Adha.

Id-ul-Adha

This festival marks the end of the pilgrimage or Hajj. It is celebrated by all Muslims and not just those who make the pilgrimage. It is a reminder of the willingness of Ibrahim to sacrifice his son for God. Because of this, a lamb or sheep is sacrificed and the meat is shared among the family, neighbours and the poor. Cards and presents are exchanged – which makes it a popular festival among Muslim children.

Ashura

In the year 680 CE, the people of Kufa (in what is now Iraq) invited Husain, the son of the *khalifah* Ali, to be their new ruler. Husain set off with 70 followers and his family but they were attacked by their opponents at a place called Kerbala on the banks of the River Euphrates, south of what is now Baghdad.

Husain and his followers were starved of food and water for ten days before being killed. Every year, in the Islamic month of Muharram, those Muslims (known as Shi'ahs or Shi'ites) who believe he was the rightful leader of all Muslims make a pilgrimage to Kerbala.

Ashura is a day of fasting, when Shi'ahs remember the martyrdom of Husain ibn Ali. The majority of Muslims (known as Sunni Muslims) do not observe Ashura, some even believing it to be 'haram', or forbidden.

Chinese Muslims here celebrate Id-ul-Fitr with their own local foods, including traditional sweets and cakes.

The Shrine of Husain ibn Ali in Kerbala, Iraq.

Muslims are divided as to whether Islam needs to become more 'modern' or more traditional.

Sunni and Shi'ah

All Muslims agree on the main parts of their faith. They believe they follow the teachings of the Prophet and believe that the Qur'an shows them the way to live. As in most religions, however, there are different groups.

Following the death of the Prophet Muhammad, Abu Bakr was chosen to be the Muslim leader or *khalifah*. His followers became known as Sunni Muslims. Nowadays about 90 per cent of Muslims belong to this group.

Those who had supported Ali (who did indeed become the second *khalifah*) wanted all future leaders to come from the Prophet's family (as did Ali). These supporters became known as Shi'ahs or members of the *Shi'at-Ali* ('the party of Ali'). Some Shi'ahs believe it is right to fight for what they believe, even if it means being killed themselves. They live mainly in Iran and southern Iraq.

Look it Up

28 ☾ Conflicts and Convictions

For 800 years, Muslims led the world in science and learning, making new inventions and discoveries. Then many Muslim countries gradually lost their power and were taken over by Western nations.

After several centuries, many Muslims became convinced they should return to the teachings of the Qur'an and live much stricter lives – and regain their independence. This began to happen in 1926 when the Islamic kingdom of Saudi Arabia came into being. Since the Second World War, other Muslim countries have regained their independence.

Islam in the Modern World

For Muslims, Islam guides all their actions and sayings. This is sometimes difficult for non-Muslims to understand. Some decide that all Muslims are too 'serious' or fanatical about their faith; that they are all 'fundamentalists'.

Some Muslims have indeed turned against the West because they regard some Western customs as sinful. Others think that Western countries have behaved badly towards them by invading their countries. Because of this, they want to make Islam stronger by following the teachings of Islam ever more strictly.

A few Muslims have even become terrorists in their fight against Western values. Most Muslims oppose terrorism, however.

Iranian schoolgirls wearing Islamic dress.

Women in Islam

Islam teaches that men and women are equally important but different. While men usually work outside the home, women look after the home and the family. But women do have equal rights to own property and to be educated. They can also take jobs outside the home – often working as teachers or in hospitals.

These freedoms vary from country to country. In some, women can become politicians. In others, they are still not allowed to drive cars. Many Muslims now admit that women have not always been granted the rights promised them in the Qur'an.

Dress

The Qur'an also teaches that both 'men and women should lower their gaze and to be mindful of their chastity' (Surah 24:30–31). This means that they should also dress modestly.

Because of this, men usually keep themselves covered at least from the waist to the knees. Some Muslims believe the rule means women must keep their head covered in front of men to whom they are not related. Stricter Muslims believe they should be covered from head to foot, showing only their wrists, feet and face – and in some cases only their eyes.

Twice Prime Minister of Pakistan, Benazir Bhutto was an example of a woman who could wield power and influence.

Caring for the World

One day, the Prophet Muhammad wanted to wear a certain cloak. When he found it, his cat was sleeping on it with her kittens. Rather than disturb them, the Prophet cut off the end of the cloak they were sleeping on – and left them there sleeping in peace. He made do with the part of the cloak that remained.

Many centuries later, a Muslim called Ibn abd as-Salam created the first statement of animal rights.

Islam has always taught that men and women should care for the world, the environment, the animals and plant life. It teaches that creation is not owned by humans but given to them on trust, by God. One day they will have to account for the way they have looked after it.

Women in Afghanistan wearing hijabs.

Many of the world faiths have their roots in the same part of the world.

The Mother Goddess

One of the gods worshipped in the cities of Mohenjo-Daro and Harappa seems to have been a mother goddess, Mahadevi. She was respected as a creator of life and goddess of agriculture. She is still worshipped by Hindus in her own form and in the form of goddesses such as Lakshmi.

An ancient statue of a goddess found in the Indus valley.

Look it Up

29 🌳 Religions of the East

The land once called Mesopotamia (much of it now called Iraq) and its great cities of Babylon and Ur was the original source of the monotheistic, Ibrahamic faiths: Judaism, Christianity and Islam.

The 'next-door' country, Iran (once called Persia), was home to another, ancient monotheistic religion, Zoroastrianism – and also (much later) to the Bahá'í faith. The great river valley to the east of Iran saw the birth and development of the great religions of the East.

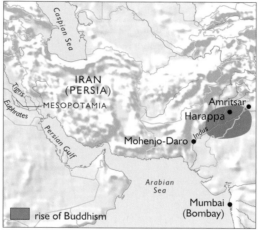

The birthplace of Hinduism, Buddhism and, later, Sikhism.

The Valley of the Indus

The River Indus flows from the Himalayan mountains down to the Arabian Sea. Long before the world faiths that are followed today, another important civilization flourished in this valley.

Two of its cities were Mohenjo-Daro and Harappa, which lay in what is now Pakistan.

From excavations that began in 1921 CE, it is known that these cities were of enormous size for their time, with populations of about 30,000. They had highly efficient sanitation systems and their paved streets were laid out on a grid pattern (like those of modern New York). The houses were built of bricks (all of the same size) and had thick, windowless walls to keep the rooms cool.

It was from this area that Hinduism and, later, Buddhism were to spread throughout the Indian subcontinent – and further afield.

The remains of an ancient city in the Indus valley with a newer Buddhist stupa in the background.

✦ Zoroastrianism

Zoroastrianism is both one of the oldest religious faiths in the world and a living faith with followers mainly in Iran and also in India, where they are known as Parsis. It was one of the first religions, possibly the first, to teach there was only one God.

Zarathustra

The founder of Zoroastrianism was a man called Zarathustra (also known as Zoroaster). It is not certain when he lived but it was possibly around the year 1200 BCE. He was born in what is now north-east Iran and is said to have been the only baby that laughed when he was born rather than cry.

At about the age of 30, he had a series of visions from what he described as 'the Supreme God': Ahura Mazda, the creator of all life and goodness. Zarathustra taught that Ahura Mazda was helped by the *Amesha Spentas,* or angels. He also taught that there was an evil power, Angra Mainyu, who would eventually be destroyed by goodness. His other teachings included the coming of a saviour, a day of judgment and a belief in life after death.

Zoroastrian beliefs in angels, judgment, heaven and hell are thought to have influenced both Judaism (when the Jews were exiled in Babylon) and, much later, Christianity.

Zoroastrians pray five times a day, as do followers of Islam.

Look it Up

7 The Promised Land
19 Festivals and Holy Days
24 The Five Pillars

The Parsis

When Muslims gained power in Persia, they began to make life difficult for the Zoroastrians. Eventually many of them migrated from Persia in 937 CE to north-western India, where they became known as Parsis.

At first, the local prince, Prince Jadi Ranah, denied them entry. Tactfully he sent their leader a bowl full of milk, filled to the brim, as a sign that there was no room for them in his princedom. The leader of the Parsis took some sugar and dissolved it in the milk. The milk didn't overflow. He returned it to Jadi Ranah. The prince realized what was meant by their reply: they could fit into his land. He admitted the Parsis, they quickly integrated – and (just as the sugar sweetened the milk) so the Parsis are said to have 'sweetened' or improved the economy around Mumbai.

The Zoroastrian Naujote ceremony, also observed by modern-day Parsis, when children become adult members of their faith.

> Hindus believe that God is neither male nor female but a great Spirit that cannot be imagined: Brahman.

The Salt in the Water

A young man called Svetaketu once asked his father how God can be everywhere yet we cannot see him. This is what his father told him: 'Place this salt in water, my son, and return tomorrow.'

The young man did as he was told. The next morning, his father said to him, 'Bring me the salt.'

The young man looked in the water but could not find the salt for it had dissolved. His father then said, 'Taste the water. How is it?'

'It's salty.'

'Taste it from the other side.'

'It's salty.'

'So where is the salt?'

'I can't see it.'

His father then said, 'In the same way, you cannot see the Spirit. But in truth the Spirit is everywhere.'

The Chandogya Upanishad 6. 12–14

A Hindu holy man washes in the waters of the River Ganga in northern India.

30 ॐ The Beginnings of Hinduism

From its origins in the fertile valley of the River Indus with its ancient civilizations, Hinduism has grown into the world's third largest religion. It has over 900 million followers worldwide. It is also one of the world's oldest religions but it has many differing beliefs and had no one founder or teacher.

It has been compared to a river, fed by many streams. Each stream has its own source. Out of this variety of beginnings (which can be traced back over 4,000 years) slowly grew present-day beliefs.

The Name of the Faith

Its name comes from the River Indus, which once formed the boundary between India and Persia (now Iran). Indus was the name given to the river by the Ancient Greeks – who also gave the name India to the land beyond the Indus. The river was originally known simply as *Sindhu*, a word from an ancient Asian language called Sanskrit, meaning 'river'. Unable to pronounce this Sanskrit word, the Persians called it the Hindu. Today, many Hindus do not use the word 'Hindu'. They call their religion *sanatan dharma,* which means 'everlasting truth'.

Dharma

'Dharma' also means 'duty': the duty that every person has to live their own life well. This includes worship, doing one's best while at work and not hurting other people or animals. Dharma is different for each person. It depends on the person, what they are good at and the conditions in which they are born.

Doing their dharma to the best of their ability is a main aim in life for every person who follows Hinduism.

Hindus outside a temple of the Hindu god Vishnu, the walls of which are decorated with huge, elaborate stone carvings. Behind the women is one wheel of the god's chariot.

Reincarnation

There is a widespread belief throughout India that, after one life, all living things are born into another life: they are 'reincarnated'. This belief in a continuing cycle of birth, death and rebirth is called 'samsara' and is shared by both Hindus and Buddhists.

They believe that, after one life, a person's soul – or 'atman' – passes into a new life. What form this new life takes depends on how the previous life was lived.

During a lifetime, a person builds up 'karma', the effect of deeds done in this life. If that life has been full of wrongdoing, the karma is bad and the atman is reborn in a lowly form – perhaps as an animal. If the wrongdoing has been only moderately bad, rebirth will be as a humble human being.

Hindus believe that, at birth, memories of previous lives are lost. When innocent or good people suffer in life, Hindus believe it is because of sins being carried over from a previous life. Hindus also believe that karma is automatic, a law of nature.

The final aim is 'moksha': the release from the cycle of death and rebirth. It is achieved by overcoming ignorance and desires.

Look it Up

32 Hindu Holy Writings
34 Being a Hindu
57 New Religious Movements

Hinduism has millions of gods but only one God.

The goddess Durga destroys the buffalo demon.

The Mother Goddess

The mother goddess or 'great goddess', Mahadevi, has many forms and is often pictured with many arms.

Mahadevi sometimes takes the form of Durga, who is always accompanied by a lion or tiger. Durga is a destroyer – but a destroyer only of what is evil.

In particular, Durga is the destroyer of a mighty buffalo demon called Mahishasura, which could be killed only by a woman. The battle between them lasted nine days and nights but eventually Durga thrust her trident into the monster's chest.

Besides being a destroyer, Durga is also tender and protective.

In eastern India, her festival is known as Durga Puja. In western and northern India, the festival is known as Navaratri, meaning 'nine nights'.

31 ॐ One God or Many Gods

Hindus believe that the great Spirit or God, Brahman, who brought everything into being, has no form or shape and cannot be seen. Because many people need a god they can feel close to; a god they can picture in their minds and worship, Brahman can take the form of a personal god such as Vishnu – or a goddess such as Lakshmi.

Hinduism has many 'personal' gods besides Brahman. Indeed, Hinduism has been said to have 330 million gods.

For many Hindus, the most important god is Shiva, the Lord of the Dance of Time.

For many other Hindus, the most important god is Vishnu.

For a third group of Hindus, the mother goddess is seen as being more important and stronger than any of the gods.

Almost all Hindus have a favourite god and may have a special shrine to that god in their home.

The Hindu symbol for God or Brahman is Aum or Om, said as 'ohh-m' and written like this.

Vishnu

Vishnu is often worshipped in one of the different forms he has taken when he has come to earth. These 'forms' or shapes are named 'avatars' and are said to happen either to prevent a great evil or to perform goodness on earth. Nine of Vishnu's avatars are said to have already appeared.

The god Vishnu shown seated on a many-headed serpent.

A.Giringer

Lith. de Marlet et C?? rue de Bondy, ??

A young Hindu carries a symbol of Ganesha during a ten-day festival in honour of the god near New Delhi, India.

Two of the most important are in the forms of Rama and Krishna. Another, later, avatar was in the form of the Buddha. It is said a tenth avatar will happen when this earth is at the end of its life. Vishnu's tenth avatar will then destroy the world and recreate it.

Ganesha

Another popular god is Ganesha, Shiva's son. Hindus believe that Shiva accidentally cut Ganesha's head off. When he saw what had happened, Shiva was so upset he promised he would replace the head with the head of the first living thing he saw – which was an elephant.

For Hindus, Ganesha is the god of learning and of good luck. Hindus often pray to him when they are starting something new – and ask that he will bring them success.

The Lord of Time

Hindus call the night of each new moon Shivaratri, 'the night of Shiva'. One 'new moon night' (which occurs in either February or March) is even more special because it is Shiva's birthday, Mahashivatri, and on this night Shiva performed the dance of creation. This is why he is also called the Lord of the Dance.

In the statue of his eternal dance, Shiva is treading ignorance underfoot and the circle of flame is the cycle of time.

In temples across India, people fast and young women offer gifts of dairy products, fruits and vegetables as they worship Shiva – in the hope that he will bless them with good husbands.

During the night, a symbol of Shiva is bathed in a continuous stream of milk until dawn when the fast is broken and worshippers eat the gifts they have brought to the temple.

Shiva, the Lord of the cycle of creation – life and death.

Look it Up

29 Religions of the East
30 The Beginnings of Hinduism
35 Hindu Festivals

**Hinduism has many
different collections of
holy writings.**

Teachings from the Upanishads

There are many sayings in the 'Upanishads' about samsara, the cycle of birth, death and rebirth:

Just as a caterpillar, when it comes to the end of a blade of grass, reaches out to another blade of grass and draws itself over to it; so the Soul, leaving one body and unwisdom behind, reaches out to another body and draws itself over to it.

This quote comes from a section of the Upanishads known as 'The Supreme Teaching'.

Hindus believe that one of the ways to moksha (release from samsara) is by yoga and meditation. From the Svetasvatara Upanishad:

The first fruits of yoga are health, little waste matter and a clear complexion; lightness of the body … and an absence of greedy desires… Then the soul of man becomes a lamp by which he finds the truth of Brahman.

Part of a wall painting in Madurai, India, showing the story of the Ramayana. In Indian paintings, gods and goddesses are often coloured blue as a sign they are not earthly beings.

32 ॐ Hindu Holy Writings

Hinduism does not have just one holy book. The very earliest writings or texts are the 'Vedas'. The word *veda* means 'knowledge' and Hindus believe that the Vedas were revealed directly by Brahman. There are four Vedas, containing hymns (or songs), prayers and instructions. The most famous Veda is the 'Rig Veda' – 'song of knowledge' – and it contains 1,028 different hymns in praise of the gods and about the creation of the world.

Another group of holy texts is called the 'Upanishads'. The Upanishads and the Vedas are called *shruti* – meaning 'they were heard': wise men are believed to have heard them directly from Brahman.

The Upanishads

The word *upanishad* can be very loosely translated as 'Sit down near your teacher'. These writings are about 2,500 years old and, like the Vedas (which are even older), were written down only after many centuries.

There are more than a hundred Upanishads and they explain the important beliefs of Hinduism, such as the teaching that Brahman is present everywhere and is within all living things.

Rama and Sita

Long ago, in the city of Ayodhya, there lived a prince called Rama. When his father (who was king of Ayodhya) died, jealous people forced Rama to flee the city. His beautiful wife Sita went with him and they spent 14 years living in a dark forest where they had many adventures and faced many dangers.

Once, an evil, ten-headed demon called Ravana captured Sita and carried her off to an island called Lanka. During their time in the forest, Rama had made many friends. One of them was Hanuman, the monkey god. Together with Rama, Hanuman and a great army of animals fought a terrible battle to rescue Sita. Finally, Rama was able to kill Ravana by shooting an arrow into his heart.

Rama and Sita were now able to return to Ayodhya. As they reached the outskirts of the city it was getting dark, but a woman saw them coming and lit a lamp to show them the way. Her neighbour lit another. Others placed candles in their windows to celebrate the return of the brave King Rama.

Their return and the triumph of good over evil is celebrated at the festival of Divali.

In one of the adventures told in the Ramayana, Rama and Sita escape from danger on the back of a strange bird called Garuda, a crowned bird that often transports Vishnu or fights for him.

The Mahabharata and the Ramayana

These two Hindu holy writings are known as 'smriti' ('that which is remembered'). These long poems were composed by people, remembered and passed down through history.

The Mahabharata is the world's longest poem: it is about 100,000 verses long. It tells the story of a war between two royal families. Part of it, the Bhagavad Gita ('song of the Lord'), contains many of the teachings of Hinduism and advice about daily life.

The Ramayana retells the adventures on earth of the god Rama.

These smriti texts are very popular with Hindus and are told in many ways. Today, many Hindu children learn the stories of the Mahabharata and the Ramayana from comic books.

Look it Up

'Puja', or worship, may take place in the home or in a temple (known as a *mandir*).

33 ॐ Puja and the Mandir

Hinduism teaches that Brahman is everywhere – and can be worshipped anywhere and at any time. Its holy writings also say that places of pilgrimage, river banks, caves, mountains and even trees are good places to worship. Even so, Hindus have also built special places for worship.

The Temple

A Hindu temple is often known by the Gujerati word *mandir*. In towns and cities, *mandirs* may consist of lots of smaller buildings. In small villages, the *mandir* might be just a thatched shelter. Many *mandirs* are built near rivers because rivers are thought to be holy. In Western towns where there are only a few Hindus, an ordinary house may be set aside as a *mandir*. Besides being a place of worship, it will act as a meeting place for Hindus.

Lighting lamps at home at the start of puja.

Puja in the Home

It is usual for every Hindu home to have a shrine: a tiny place of worship, with pictures and statues of the gods, often decorated with flowers or fruit. If the house is big enough, there will be a whole room set aside especially for 'puja'.

Hindus usually get up early and bathe. The mother of the family goes first to the shrine, lights a lamp and burns a little sweet-scented incense. The rest of the family then come, together or separately, to offer prayers, to meditate, to practise yoga or just to read from Hindu holy writings.

Simple gifts (such as a flower or some rice) are offered to the gods, and words from Hindu holy writings may be repeated several times. A saying repeated in this way is known as a 'mantra'. Often, Hindus simply use 'Om' as a mantra – a way of concentrating on Brahman.

If it is a specially built *mandir*, it is likely to have a domed roof.

At the doorway, there is always a place where shoes may be left. Everyone entering takes off their shoes as a mark of respect and as a sign that they are leaving the outside world behind them.

Almost every Hindu temple has a little bell. When Hindus arrive at the temple, they ring it to say that they have come to

Children offer gifts in an Indian temple, or *mandir*.

offer their prayers. They may also bring gifts of flowers or sweets for the god or goddess. Later, these are often given to the poor.

The main shrine room usually has a carpet and symbols (*murti*) or pictures of the different gods and goddesses of Hinduism. Worship is led by a 'Brahmin', or priest. Hindu priests spend many years studying and learning the *shruti* holy writings. Few Hindus can read them in their original language, Sanskrit.

Daily worship begins before sunrise. The *murti* of the main god worshipped in that *mandir* is 'woken up' and washed by the priest – just as a mother does in a Hindu home. The statue is then clothed in red and gold, and flowers may be placed on it or nearby.

For puja, the people stand or sit cross-legged. Sometimes they touch the ground with their forehead as a way of showing respect to the god or goddess. The priests may give sermons or talks explaining the Vedas and Upanishads.

During puja, *prashad* is given to the people. This food, which has received the god's blessing, is usually a mixture of fruit, nuts and sweets.

Lighting the *arti* lamps.

After puja, a small red dot may be placed on the forehead of those who have been to worship. This is called a *tilak* and its shape may show which god the person has worshipped.

A young girl has the *tilak* put on her forehead.

Arti

One part of puja in a *mandir* is the *arti* ceremony. Small lights or candles on a tray are offered to the god or goddess so that they will be blessed. The tray of lights is then carried among the people, who may put small amounts of money on the tray. More importantly, they hold their hands over the flames and then touch their eyes and forehead. In this way, they believe they are being given power from the god or goddess.

Sometimes the *arti* burns ghee (clarified butter) and has five flames.

Look it Up

31 One God or Many Gods
32 Hindu Holy Writings
34 Being a Hindu
36 Ganga Ma: Mother Ganges

The Shri Swaminarayan temple in north London.

The stages of a Hindu's life are marked by special ceremonies called 'samskars'.

34 ॐ Being a Hindu

Hindus have strong family ties. Grandparents, aunts and uncles often all live in the same family group. Together, they celebrate the different 'samskars' in each family member's life, believing each ceremony will protect him or her from any danger.

The birth of a baby in a Hindu home is a big event. Twelve days after the baby is born, a priest or member of the family welcomes it into the world by whispering its name in its ear. The whole house is decorated with leaves and flowers to mark the happy event.

Meditation

There are four paths to moksha:

- by devotion to Brahman
- by being unselfish
- by study and gaining knowledge
- by meditation and yoga.

Meditation means emptying the mind of all worries and earthly thoughts in order to concentrate on God or Brahman. This might be done by repeating a mantra or through yoga.

Yoga is the use of physical exercises to help meditation. Those who practise yoga find they can control their breathing and even slow their heartbeat.

Yoga has been taken up by many people in the West who do not consider themselves to be Hindu.

A young student of yoga demonstrates his self-control.

The Sacred Thread Ceremony

This samskar is only for boys and for those boys who are in the first three castes. It is performed some time between their seventh and twelfth birthdays. It marks their entry into adulthood and is the most important ceremony in a young Hindu's life. Before it takes place, the boy has to learn all the responsibilities of an adult Hindu.

During the ceremony, the boy and a priest sit on opposite sides of a small fire. Prayers and hymns are chanted and then the thread is put over his left shoulder. It is made in the form of a loop and is usually either red, yellow or white. The boy's responsibilities are now to:

Indian boys receive the Sacred Thread.

- worship God
- respect holy men and holy books
- honour his parents and old people
- help the poor
- care for animals and all living things.

Marriage

Hindus respect older people. This is one reason many young Hindus agree to 'arranged' marriages. They accept that their parents and older relatives have the wisdom to suggest or choose a suitable partner. In the past, the couple getting married might not even meet until the wedding day. Nowadays, they are more likely to meet beforehand and more young people are choosing their own future partners.

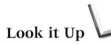

Look it Up

Sri Lankan Hindus take part in their wedding ceremony.

The ceremony lasts about an hour. The bride wears a red and gold sari and much gold jewellery. The couple sit in front of a fire lit in a special metal container and a priest recites verses from the Hindu holy writings. The most important part of the ceremony is when the bride's sari and the husband's shirt are tied together and they then walk round the fire seven times. Each time they make a promise to each other. After the wedding, the wife becomes a part of her husband's family.

Although the ceremony may take only an hour, the celebrations may go on for several days.

Funerals

All Hindus are cremated and hope their ashes will be scattered on the River Ganga (Ganges). They believe that this will save them from several future lives and hasten moksha.

A cremation ceremony on the edge of the Ganga.

Those with lowly jobs, such as basket weaving, still face discrimination.

The Caste System

For thousands of years, people in India have lived by the 'caste' system, based on the idea of samsara. People are reborn into a certain caste or class and cannot move out of it in that life. There are four main groups, or 'varnas':

• *Brahmins* (who, traditionally, were always priests but now may have other professions)
• *Kshatriyas*: rulers and soldiers
• *Vaishyas*: shopkeepers, farmers and craftsmen
• *Shudras*: ordinary workers and servants.

Outside the system were the 'harijans' (sometimes called 'untouchables'), who were thought fit to do only the dirtiest jobs. It is now against the law to class anyone as harijan. Over the centuries, the varnas have divided into smaller groups called 'jatis'. A person's jati would decide what job they did. Nowadays, children do not always do the same job as their parents – but people still know their jati and are likely to marry within it.

Hindu festivals celebrate the seasons of the year, link worship with pleasure and are times for family reunions.

Dassehra

At the end of the festival of Durga Puja comes Dassehra. In the Indian city of New Delhi, this huge wooden statue of the Demon Ravana (stuffed with fireworks) waits to be set on fire to celebrate Rama's victory over the demon – a victory of good over evil.

Holi is a 'fun' festival.

Look it Up

31 One God or Many Gods
32 Hindu Holy Writings
49 Jorhmela and Gurpurbs

35 ॐ Hindu Festivals

The three main festivals of the Hindu year are Holi, Durga Puja and Divali. Hundreds of other local and regional festivals are celebrated – in different ways in different parts of India.

The Hindu year normally has 354 days, divided into twelve months, following the phases of the moon. In some regions, the month begins with the new moon; in others it starts with the full moon. Every two or three years, an extra month is added to keep the Hindu calendar in step with the solar calendar of 365 days – and to make sure the Hindu festivals occur in the correct seasons. For all these reasons, the 'Western' dates of the different festivals vary from year to year.

Holi

Holi (in March or April) marks the end of winter, the celebration of spring and the new year. Bonfires are lit the night before the five-day festival in the belief they will disperse evil spirits. The next morning, water pistols, plastic bottles and bicycle pumps are all used to squirt water which has been brightly coloured with powder all over anyone within reach – never mind their age, sex or class. This is in memory of how the god Krishna played tricks on people when he was young.

Durga Puja

This nine-day festival falls in either September or October and celebrates the victory of good over evil. In east India and Bangladesh, it celebrates especially the story of how the goddess Durga slew the buffalo demon. It is also known as Navaratri.

For Hindus, the nine nights of Durga Puja are a time for dancing and music, plays, shopping, feasting and fireworks. It is a time when women wear their newest and brightest clothes and it is supposed to be a good time for buying gold or starting new projects – but for young people it is the nightly feasting and dancing that matter most.

In many areas, barley grains (or seeds of nine different plants) are sown in pots of mud, and watered and blessed daily.

At Dassehra (meaning 'the tenth day'), statues of Durga are taken to a river and washed. As the statues disappear under the water, the river carries away all unhappiness and bad luck – and the pots of seedlings are given to family and friends as a blessing.

In southern India, the festival celebrates the story of the Ramayana.

In northern India, wooden statues of a demon king, Ravana, are built out of wood and paper. Ones in New Delhi are 30 metres high. They are packed with fireworks and, at Dassehra, they are set alight when an actor shoots a blazing arrow into them.

Ratha Yatra

This festival occurs in May or June and the most famous celebrations are held in Puri in the state of Orissa on the eastern coast of India.

The people of Puri build three huge chariots, 13 metres high and shaped like temples on wheels. It takes 400 men to pull each one in procession through the streets. On the chariots and sheltered by red and gold canopies are statues of the Hindu god Krishna (who is also known as Lord Jagannath or 'the Lord of the Universe') and his brother Balaram and sister Subhadra.

At the end of a week, during which the statues are kept in a garden temple, the chariots are broken up and the wood is distributed to the many pilgrims who come to Puri for the festival and to temple kitchens to be used as fuel.

Indian children light tiny lamps at Divali.

Divali

This celebration of hope, friendship and goodwill may extend over five days, is held in honour of Rama and occurs in either October or November.

It recalls how Rama triumphed over evil and how light triumphs over darkness. The celebration of his return with Sita to Ayodha is called Divali or *Deepavali,* which means 'a row of lamps'. Many Hindus believe Lakshmi, the goddess of wealth, visits every home where a row of lights is burning and brings good luck.

Homes are cleaned at the start of the festival. As dusk falls, lamps are lit in every room and outside in the porch or garden. Weather permitting, windows are left open to welcome in Lakshmi. People exchange Divali cards and gifts of sweets (especially milky and coconut ones). Fireworks are lit and shops and town centres are decorated.

For Hindus, the River Ganga is the most holy river in the world.

Pilgrimage

Many people go to hear their favourite musicians rather than just listen to recordings, or travel to watch a particular team play in real life rather than just see them on television.

In a similar way, followers of some faiths feel it is good actually to journey to places that are important in their religion. Such journeys are called pilgrimages.

Until modern transport was available, pilgrimages meant much hardship. Even so, pilgrims went on such journeys for many reasons:

- to prove their sorrow for wrongdoings
- to pay respect to another follower of their faith
- to seek healing
- to gain peace of mind.

For Hindus, a pilgrimage is a way of improving one's karma.

36 ॐ Ganga Ma: Mother Ganges

Hindus do not *have* to go on pilgrimages but many do – as a way of celebrating their faith. They may undertake a pilgrimage to give thanks for blessings or good fortune they have received, or as a way of praying for a sick child or relative. The most frequent reason is because Hindus believe their wrongdoings (or sins) will be washed away if they bathe in one of India's many holy rivers.

People who are well-off may travel by plane, train or bus. Others walk, often for long distances. A group of villagers, once their crops have been harvested, may make a pilgrimage together in a bullock cart. Very holy people test themselves by walking barefoot. However they travel, most enjoy the journey. It is a chance to meet friends, wear new clothes and eat festive meals, because pilgrimages are often made at the time of festivals.

Pilgrimages are made to many different places in India and they are usually cheerful places with shops selling locally made items, traders bargaining and many street entertainments. One of the greatest centres for pilgrimage is Varanasi, which stands on the holy River Ganga where it is joined by the River Varuna. The Ganga (known as Ganges in English) is also said to be a goddess called Ganga – and so is sometimes called 'Ganga Ma' or 'Mother Ganges'.

The river has its source in a glacier in the Himalayan mountains and flows south-east through northern India and then through Bangladesh and into the Indian Ocean. Pilgrimages are made to many points on the Ganga.

A party of pilgrims trek through the Himalayan mountains in northern India.

A cow wanders where it chooses in the city of Gaitor in the north-western state of Rajasthan, India.

Varanasi

Varanasi is also known as Benares. The god Shiva is said to have made this place his home on earth.

Here, for about three miles, one bank of the Ganga is lined with steps known as 'ghats'. From these ghats, the pilgrims bathe in their thousands. The women are dressed in saris, the men usually in loin cloths. They enter the river, let the water cover them and then drink it by taking it in their cupped hands. Not only is this believed to carry away a person's sins (from their present life and from earlier ones) and so hasten moksha, but taking bottles of the water home for those unable to make the pilgrimage is believed to bring blessings.

Look it Up

26 Living a Muslim Life (Al Hajj)
30 The Beginnings of Hinduism
31 One God or Many Gods

The Cow

Hindus never harm but always show special respect to cows because they are givers of milk, a symbol of life itself. Others think cows should be respected because, in times gone by, they were a measure of wealth. In India, cows are allowed to wander where they like. If a person kills or injures a cow, that person can be put in prison.

No Hindus eat beef and many Hindus eat no meat at all.

Pilgrims bathe from 'ghats' on the banks of the Ganga in Varanasi.

Ruled by Mughals

In 1525, the army of a Muslim people called the Mughals (sometimes spelled Moghuls or Moguls) marched into northern India. The next year, their leader, a man called Babur, imposed his rule on most of northern India. A tolerant Sunni Muslim, he traded with the rest of the Muslim world but encouraged the building of Hindu temples and made peace with the Hindu kingdoms of southern India.

Later Mughal rulers (such as the emperor Akbar) believed that Hindus, Muslims, Jains, Parsis and Christians should all be treated equally. A later Mughal emperor, Aurangzeb (who ruled from 1658 to 1707 CE), thought differently. He invaded the Hindu kingdoms in central and southern India, imposed strict Islamic law and tore down hundreds of Hindu temples. Following his death in 1707, the British (with the help of Hindu leaders) gradually gained control of all India.

Look it Up

37 ॐ Hinduism in India – and Around the World

For over a thousand years, Hinduism in its various forms was the main religion in India. Then, about 2,500 years ago, some Indians began to follow the teachings of the Buddha. Christianity may have reached India soon after the time of Jesus. Many centuries later, when Muslims invaded India, Islam also became an important religion. From then, there were often conflicts between Hindus and Muslims. Just over 500 years ago, a new faith, Sikhism, developed in north-west India. In the fifteenth and sixteenth centuries, Christian missionaries journeyed to India.

Historic India is now divided into India, Pakistan and Bangladesh.

Indian Independence

During the nineteenth century, India became part of the British empire but from about the year 1885 onwards, many Indians began to want independence. This was achieved in 1947 but only by dividing India into two countries – India and Pakistan. India remained largely Hindu but Pakistan became a Muslim country. This division resulted in many people moving from one country to another and there was much fighting and bloodshed. There has been continuing tension between India and Pakistan.

Pakistan later divided into two largely Muslim countries, Pakistan and Bangladesh.

Despite the troubles, Hinduism remains a mainly peaceful religion and about 80 per cent of the Indian population regard themselves as Hindu.

A typical sight in present-day India: the temple elephant carries a symbol of the local god around the village.

The Venkateswara Temple at Tividale in the West Midlands, England, is the largest Hindu temple in Europe.

Mahatma Gandhi

Born in 1869 in western India, Mohandas Gandhi was a shy, nervous boy. Even so, he married at the age of 14 and at 18 went to London to study to be a lawyer. In 1893, he went to work in South Africa. There, he was thrown out of a railway carriage because he had the 'wrong' colour skin.

Gandhi set about working to help Indians in South Africa and to change the race laws. He did this by non-violent protests but even so was put in prison three times. In 1915, he returned to India.

When some English soldiers killed 400 Indians in Amritsar, Gandhi started working for Indian independence by staging hunger strikes and peaceful protests. He was often arrested and sent to prison. He also worked to help the 'untouchables', giving them their new name, harijans ('children of God').

When India became independent, Gandhi (a Hindu) worked to help Muslims still living in India – but was killed by another Hindu in 1948. His ashes were scattered on the River Ganga.

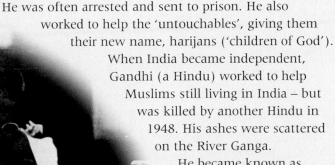

He became known as Mahatma Gandhi ('mahatma' means 'great soul'). He made his own simple cotton clothes, practised yoga, and his favourite books were the Bhagavad Gita and the Christian New Testament.

Hindus Abroad

In the 1800s, many Indian workers moved abroad to find work – many going to South Africa. Many more Indians moved abroad from the 1960s onwards, settling especially in cities in the United States of America, Canada, the United Kingdom and Singapore.

In these countries, Hindu temples were opened and became important meeting places. Some rivers in western countries have become 'holy' and women have begun to play a greater part in teaching the faith – but some young Hindus in the West are not always so happy to follow Hindu traditions.

In recent years, numbers of Americans and Europeans who are not descended from Indians have turned to Hinduism. Many have become followers of particular teachers or gurus and have been attracted by Hindu teachings about peace and non-violence.

Buddhism began in
northern India about
2,500 years ago.

Bodhi Day

The day of the Buddha's enlightenment is celebrated mainly by Buddhists in Japan but also by Buddhists in Nepal and northern India as 'Bodhi Day'.

On this day, those who follow the teachings of the Buddha wish each other *Budu saranai!* It means 'May the peace of the Buddha be yours.' This is a reminder that the prince found peace by sitting under a fig tree, since known as a bo or bodhi tree.

On Bodhi Day, many Buddhists send greetings cards to one another – like this one of the Buddha under the bodhi tree.

Look it Up

38 ✴ The Prince and the Truth

Siddhartha Gautama was a Hindu prince who lived from about 560 to 480 BCE. His father tried to protect him from any knowledge of suffering. Siddhartha left home to find out what life was really like.

Eventually, he began to understand what was truly important. For him, finding truth was like coming out of darkness into light. For that reason, he became known as the Buddha, which means 'the enlightened one' or 'the one who is awake'.

The Story of Siddhartha

Prince Siddhartha had lived all his life in a palace and had everything he wanted. Servants did whatever he said. Even so, he was bored. One day he said, 'This palace is a paradise. The rooms are as brilliant as rain clouds in autumn. But I wish I could make a journey outside the palace, to see what the world is really like.'

After some time, his father, who was the king, agreed. Siddhartha went on a journey by royal chariot. On that journey, he saw something he had never seen before: a very old man, with a wrinkled face and bent back, bent almost nose to knee. He asked the servant driving the chariot a question. 'That man there. What's the matter with him?'

'He is old, my lord,' said the charioteer. 'Old age does that to everyone.'

'I did not realize how age destroys beauty and youth and strength,' said Siddhartha.

Next day, the prince made another journey. He saw another person at the roadside.

'What is the matter with that man?' he asked.

'That, my lord, is a leper.'

'Is that what people call disease?'

'That is what disease can do to a man.'

A statue of the Buddha as he might have looked at the time of his search for understanding.

The prince made a third journey. This time he saw a group of men weeping as they carried the body of their friend.

'What is that?' he asked.

'That, my lord,' said the charioteer, 'is a dead body.'

Saddened by all that he had seen, the prince made a fourth journey. This time he saw a holy man whose body seemed to be no more than skin and bones.

That night, on his return, the prince decided to give up his wealth, jewels and rich clothes, to leave the palace and his wife, and to live as a wandering hermit, trying to understand why there should be suffering in the world.

For the next five years, he wandered the countryside. He lived very simply, eating as little as possible – just a mouthful of pea soup or a handful of grain. He became very thin.

One day, in his search to understand what life was all about, he came to a great fig tree. 'I shall sit beneath this tree and, though my flesh and bones may waste away and my life-blood shall dry, I shall not move again until I have found the truth,' he said.

As Siddhartha sat under the tree, he suddenly knew he must teach people what he had learned. From that time onwards, he became known as the Buddha. He travelled the country with a new purpose, teaching what he now knew was the 'Truth'.

For Buddhists, the lotus flower is a symbol of enlightenment: the plant has its roots in mud but from its roots blossoms a beautiful flower.

The Four Noble Truths

The Buddha taught his followers 'The Four Noble Truths':

• In this world, nothing lasts. Even the happiest moments pass away: happiness does not last for ever. The Buddhist word for this 'unsatisfactoriness' of life is *duhkha* (a word which means 'restlessness' or 'suffering').

• *Duhkha* happens because people want more and more things and are never satisfied. They become greedy and selfish.

• But *duhkha* can cease if you overcome your selfishness, greed and hatred.

• The way to do this is to follow the Eightfold Path – which is the path all Buddhists try to follow.

A Buddhist monk from Thailand teaches children under the fig (or bodhi) tree in Bodh Gaya, India, where the Buddha is said to have found enlightenment.

Buddhism is a way of understanding the world and what happens in it.

Daily Life

Buddhists often make five promises (known as the Five Precepts), based on the teachings of the Buddha:

• not to kill or harm any living thing
• not to take anything that is not given to you
• not to indulge yourself physically
• not to lie or say anything cruel
• not to drink alcohol or take drugs.

Because Buddhists believe it is wrong to kill, most are vegetarians.

Look it Up

39 ✹ Following the Path

The Buddha was 35 years old at the time of his enlightenment. He spent the rest of his life (until he was 80) walking around India, teaching the Four Noble Truths and good ways of living.

He began his teaching at the Hindu holy city of Varanasi in a deer park at Sarnath, which is on the edge of the city. Like Hindus, the Buddha believed that after death we are born again into a new life, or 'reincarnated'. He drew a wheel on the ground and taught that life (like a circle) is never-ending. People move round from birth to death – and then back to birth again.

To make this journey as satisfactory or pleasant as possible, he said it was necessary to follow the 'Eightfold Path'.

The Eightfold Path

The Buddha taught his followers that, if they were to follow the Eightfold Path, they must take eight steps. That is, they must try to do eight things in the right or proper way.

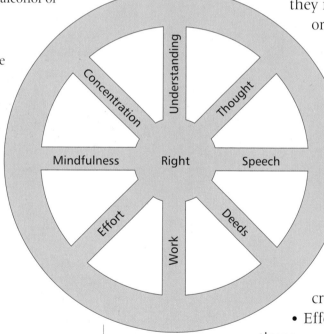

• Understanding: People should try to see clearly what they are doing with their lives.
• Thought: People should not waste time daydreaming.
• Speech: When they talk, people should say good things, not bad or cruel things.
• Deeds: Good deeds are unselfish ones: people should not be selfish.
• Work: People should try not to take jobs which will harm other living creatures.
• Effort: People should try their best at all times.
• Mindfulness: People should pay full attention to what they are doing.
• Concentration: People should try to concentrate on what they have to do.

One way of picturing the Eightfold Path is to draw eight spokes in the wheel of life – which is how the eight-spoked wheel became the symbol of Buddhism.

Buddhist Writings

In the years after the Buddha died, his followers repeated his teachings so that they would not be forgotten. It was not until some 400 years after his death that they were written down.

An Indian painting of the Buddha teaching his followers.

One set of writings is called the Tipitaka. This word means 'three baskets'. It has this name because it was first written on pages made from palm leaves which were kept in three baskets. The Tipitaka is written in a language called Pali, which was probably spoken by the Buddha. Most other Buddhist scriptures are written in an ancient Indian language called Sanskrit. Unlike monks, ordinary Buddhists rarely read these writings in their original language because they do not understand Sanskrit or Pali, but most Buddhist scriptures have been translated into other languages.

A monk in Tibet studies Buddhist holy writings.

Dharma Day

Following his enlightenment, the Buddha got up from where he had been sitting under the bodhi tree. He went to find five close friends and shared with them what Buddhists now call the Four Noble Truths. Each year, on Dharma Day, Buddhists give thanks that the Buddha shared his teaching.

This festival, celebrating the start of Buddhism, is observed especially in southern Asian countries and in the West. On this day there are often readings from the Buddhist scriptures and a chance to think about their meaning.

Learning the Way

In some Asian countries, elephants are used as transport or to carry or pull heavy loads. The Buddha once pointed out that you cannot teach a wild elephant to do this. In order to train it, it has to be harnessed to a tame one – and it will learn by copying the tame one. The Buddha went on to say that his followers should follow and copy a teacher or wise person they trusted and respected – and in that way they too would become trustworthy and respected.

Buddhists go to
temples to meditate
or to honour the
Buddha.

Meditation

The Buddha taught people to
meditate. This is not just
another word for thinking, but
a way of letting the mind grow
still and gain a sense of peace.

To meditate, a person needs
to be sitting comfortably, in a
relaxed position. The person
should then try to *stop* thinking
about everyday things and to
let their mind relax. To do this,
he or she often tries to
concentrate on one thing, such
as a pebble, a flower or a leaf,
and not let any other thoughts
come into the mind.

All the time, the person
meditating breathes slowly,
feeling the breath entering and
leaving the body and allowing
the mind to reach a state of
peace.

40 ✹ Temples and Shrines

In Bodh Gaya, the birthplace of Buddhism, the
tallest building is the Mahabodhi Temple. It stands
at the exact spot where it is believed the Buddha
received enlightenment. Inside is a huge golden
statue of the Buddha. It is about 1,700 years old.
Nearby, there are many other beautiful temples.
Many Buddhists make special journeys, or
pilgrimages, to meditate here, to light candles,
burn incense or lay flowers in front of the statues
in honour of the Buddha.

The Mahabodhi Temple.

Also to be found in India are mounds or
buildings that mark the burial places of people
important in Buddhism. These are known as 'stupas'. Other stupas
were built to mark special places in Buddhist history and are often
dome-shaped. Many are solid: they are not buildings that can be
entered.

A monk prays in front of the Bodnath
Stupa in Nepal. As the prayer flags flutter
in the wind, they are said to spread
prayers for good luck, happiness and
long life around the world.

A monk meditates in front of a footprint
preserved in stone and said to have
been made by the Buddha.

A Buddhist pagoda in Japan.

In China and Japan, Buddhist shrines are usually tall buildings called 'pagodas'.

In Thailand, Buddhist temples are called 'wats'. Almost every town has its own wat, which is cared for by local monks.

Inside a Temple

In every Buddhist temple, there will be at least one statue or carving of the Buddha. An area round this statue is known as a shrine.

There is no special day of the week when Buddhists go to a temple but many make a special visit each month at the time of the full moon. Some will take flowers or burn incense to show respect to the Buddha. They may sit or kneel near the shrine to meditate. They may bow to the statue or even lie flat on the floor – again as a way of showing respect to the Buddha. Sometimes there are processions round the temple.

Many Buddhists chant words from the scriptures to help them meditate.

In Tibetan temples (or 'wats') there may be prayer wheels. These prayer 'wheels' are drums with paper scrolls inside. Thousands of prayers are written down on the scrolls. Buddhists believe that when the wheel or drum is spun round, the prayers will be released into the world.

A Buddhist woman in the mountainous kingdom of Bhutan spins a prayer wheel.

Look it Up

34 Being a Hindu (Meditation)
38 The Prince and the Truth
41 Living as a Monk
51 Religion in China

A Religion Without God

Buddhism is sometimes described as a 'religion without a god'. Because of this, some people say it is not a religion at all but simply a way of life or a way of thinking; what is termed a 'philosophy'.

Even though Buddhists do not believe in a divine being, they believe in something 'uncreated, timeless and formless'. Because they do not believe in a god, they do not say prayers to God. Some Buddhists say prayers to that part of the 'spirit of the Buddha' which they believe is in each of us.

The Buddha never claimed to be anything but a man. After his enlightenment, he was asked a question by one of his monks:

Monk: Are you a god?
The Buddha: No.
Monk: Are you an angel?
The Buddha: No.
Monk: Are you a saint?
The Buddha: No.
Monk: Then what are you?
The Buddha: I am awake.

Nuns in Buddhism

The Buddha taught that men and women are equal and could both become enlightened. Even so, he was at first against the idea of women becoming nuns in the way that some men became monks.

However, women were encouraged by the Buddha's stepmother to become nuns, or *bhikshunis*. There are now no ordained nuns in Theravada Buddhism but there are in Mahayana Buddhism. The rules for nuns are much stricter than those for monks.

Monks and nuns in India concentrate as they listen to a sermon.

41 ⊛ Living as a Monk

After his enlightenment, the Buddha lived as a monk. His closest followers lived the same life and journeyed throughout India with the Buddha, teaching the Eightfold Path and showing by their example how life should be lived. This 'brotherhood' of monks, or *bhikshus*, became known as the 'sangha'.

Although the title 'the Buddha' usually refers to the founder of the Buddhist way of life, the title 'buddha' can be given to anyone who has gained enlightenment. Most Buddhists believe there were other buddhas in the past and that there will be more in the future.

Monastic Rules

Besides following the Five Promises, or Precepts, by which all Buddhists should live, Buddhist monks make a further five Precepts:

- not to eat excessively or after midday
- not to be involved in, or to watch, dancing, acting or singing
- not to use perfumes or ornaments
- not to use a comfortable bed
- not to accept (or even handle) gold or silver.

Besides all ten Precepts, monks should have no sexual relations, take no human life, not pretend to have powers they do not have and never take something that has not been given to them.

Traditionally, monks are allowed to own only eight things: their robes, a belt, a needle and thread, a razor, a begging bowl, a water strainer, a walking stick and a toothpick.

Monks in Colombo, Sri Lanka, receive gifts from Buddhist pilgrims from Thailand.

The Life of a Monk

Buddhist monks spend much of their time in meditation. They read and chant the holy writings of Buddhism and learn large parts of them by heart. They may also work as teachers and help in building hospitals and schools.

Boy Monks

In many Buddhist countries, young boys will often live the life of a monk, in a monastery, for a period of one to four months. This is to give them a good education both in ordinary school subjects and also in Buddhist teachings. In Thailand, they may do this as young as eight. More often than not, it happens when they are about eleven.

In some countries, there is a great family feast before a boy enters a monastery. The boy may then be dressed up in fine clothes to look like Siddhartha Gautama before he left his palace. Then the boy travels on a horse or elephant or in a carriage to the monastery. His hair is shaved off, he puts on the robes of a monk and then enters the monastery.

They are not strict places: the boys have time to play football and other games.

A few boys enter a monastery for life. In Tibet, a boy was traditionally able to do this at the age of eleven. In Burma (Myanmar), a boy may enter a monastery as a 'novice', or trainee, monk at any age from eight upwards. Full membership of the sangha comes when he is 20.

Boy monks (whose hair has begun to grow again) take time off from their studies to play football.

Becoming a Monk

Many stories are told about men keen to become Buddhist monks spending days waiting outside a monastery before even being interviewed by the master of the monks. This is to teach them that a monk needs to be humble.

One man is said to have waited for days. Finally, the master agreed to see him and asked, 'Why do you want to become a monk? To gain enlightenment, I suppose. Or to spend your life in meditation?'

'No,' replied the man. 'I want to help people in need.'

'You may enter,' said the master, 'but not as a monk. Only as a visitor. If you prove serious, you may be allowed to stay. Have you brought a begging bowl?'

'Why do I need a begging bowl?' asked the man. 'I thought people brought gifts of food to the monastery. I have often done so in the past.'

'That is true,' said the master. 'We are given food – but if you did not beg, how would you learn to be humble?'

Look it Up

There are two main types or 'schools' of Buddhism.

Buddhism in Tibet

Tibet was an independent Buddhist nation for more than 2,000 years. For the 300 years up to 1951, it was ruled by leaders known as Dalai Lamas. The word *dalai* means 'ocean' and *lama* means teacher. The Dalai Lama is a teacher whose wisdom is as deep as the ocean.

When one died, there was a search by wise men to find a child they believed to be a previous, reborn Dalai Lama.

In 1951, Chinese Communists invaded Tibet and attacked the Buddhist way of life. Six thousand monasteries were destroyed, 110,000 monks and nuns were killed and thousands more were made to give up their way of life.

The Chinese, who still control Tibet, have granted some freedoms in recent years, but Buddhism still struggles to survive in that country.

42 ✹ One Path, Two Ways

Today, most Buddhists live in Asia. Some live in India, where Buddhism began, but now there are more in other Asian countries. In some, such as Thailand and Sri Lanka, most of the people are Buddhists. There are also large numbers of Buddhists in other Asian countries such as China and Japan.

In the last hundred years, some people in Europe and in North America have also begun to follow Buddhist teachings.

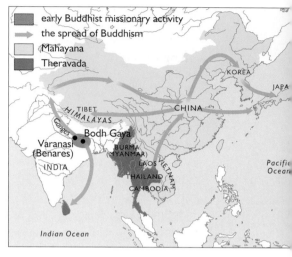

How Buddhism spread throughout East Asia.

Two Ways

Several hundred years after the death of the Buddha, there was a great gathering of Buddhist monks. At this meeting, there was some disagreement about the way Buddhist monks and nuns should live.

Over the years, Buddhists split into two groups or 'schools'. Both groups followed (and still follow) the same basic teachings, such as the importance of the Four Noble Truths, following the Eightfold Path and keeping the Five Promises or Precepts.

Pilgrims travel past strings of prayer flags, high in the Tibetan mountains.

The Escape of the Dalai Lama

By the time he was 15, the boy had become the fourteenth Dalai Lama – a ruler of Tibet. Then, in 1950, the Communist rulers of neighbouring China announced that they were going to make Tibet part of China. The powerful Chinese army invaded the peace-loving country known as 'the Land of the Snows' and set about destroying the Buddhist way of life.

For nine years, the young Dalai Lama tried to make peace with the Chinese, hoping to win freedom for his people to follow the way of the Buddha. He was determined to do this without violence because, like all Buddhists, he believed violence was always wrong.

Eventually the Tibetan people began to fear the Chinese might kidnap or kill their Dalai Lama. Many thought it best that he should leave the country, to find safety. He did not wish to leave his people but he knew that if he escaped, he could one day return and rule Tibet in peace again.

Reluctantly he decided he should leave the country. He and a small group of his followers made their plans in the greatest secrecy. They disguised themselves by not wearing their monk's robes, but the ordinary clothes of Tibetan soldiers.

They escaped at night, helped by a storm which hid the noise of their horses' hooves. Their route led up through the mountains. The paths were narrow and difficult. Heavy snow bit into their faces. Then brilliant sunlight reflected off the snow and threatened to blind those who had no goggles. They slept at night in makeshift tents and, by day, struggled on, across hills and frozen desert plains. Eventually they crossed into India and safety.

It has still not proved possible for the peace-loving Dalai Lama to return to Tibet.

In recent years, the Dalai Lama has visited many countries around the world. Here he preaches while in New Zealand.

Although they continued to agree about most things, one group or 'school' came to believe that only monks and nuns can achieve complete enlightenment and a final escape from the never-ending wheel of birth, life and death. This school of Buddhism eventually came to be known as 'early' Buddhism or Theravada Buddhism. Because of their beliefs, male Theravada Buddhists all spend some time living as monks.

The other school of Buddhism, sometimes called 'late Buddhism', follows the Mahayana tradition. Mahayana Buddhism teaches that anyone (not only monks and nuns) can achieve enlightenment and that this can be done by helping others in everyday life.

Each group has its own holy writings.

Theravada Buddhism is followed in southern Asian countries such as Thailand, Sri Lanka and Myanmar (Burma). Mahayana Buddhism is found in Tibet, China, Korea and Japan.

Look it Up

30 The Beginnings of Hinduism
   (Reincarnation)
39 Following the Path
41 Living as a Monk
43 Buddhism Today
51 Religion in China

For its followers, Buddhism continues to be a way to unselfish peace of mind and happiness.

The Buddhist Calendar

Most Buddhists, with the exception of the Japanese, use a calendar based on the movements of the moon. The dates of Buddhist festivals (and the way they are celebrated) vary from country to country, and between the different Buddhist traditions. They mark events in the Buddha's life, and one of the best known and most popular is Wesak.

A woman meditates in front of Buddhist writings in Chinese script.

Look it Up

43 ✸ Buddhism Today

One symbol of Buddhism is the lotus flower. The lotus has its roots in the mud but the flower rises above the mud to seek the sunlight. In the same way, Buddhists believe humans can rise above the troubles of the world to reach for enlightenment and understanding.

From its beginnings in India, it has become an important faith or way of life throughout South-east Asia, in China, Japan and Korea – and (in more recent times) in Western countries.

Japanese Buddhism

Buddhism reached Japan in the sixth century CE – about a thousand years after the death of the Buddha. Today, the most popular kind of Buddhism in Japan is a kind (or 'school') of Mahayana Buddhism called *Jodo Shu* or 'the Pure Land'.

Besides following all the main teachings of Buddhism, its followers honour a buddha called Amida. By meditating on his name and example, they hope to reach a heavenly or pure land called 'nirvana'. There are no monks or monasteries in this form of Buddhism.

The best known school of Buddhism in Japan is Zen Buddhism. The name Zen comes from a Chinese word for meditation.

Its followers spend time sitting cross-legged, meditating. Some will concentrate on parables or puzzles known as 'koans' in the hope they will suddenly gain new thoughts and new ideas that will lead to enlightenment.

• A man asked the Buddha, 'Without words, will you tell me truth?' The Buddha kept silent.
• A university professor came to a Zen teacher. The teacher poured tea into his visitor's cup then kept on pouring. The professor watched it overflow. 'Stop, no more will go in!' 'Like this cup', said the teacher, 'you are full of your own opinions. I cannot teach you Zen unless you first empty your cup.'
• What is the sound of one hand clapping?

A Zen Buddhist garden in Japan.

Buddhism in the West

Buddhism has been known throughout East Asia for 2,000 years. It is only in the last hundred years that it has been known in the West.

About a century ago, Westerners began to travel to the East and learned about this way of life – and shared their new ideas when they returned home. More recently, people from Tibet, Thailand and other Buddhist countries have moved west, looking for a new home, for work or to set up businesses.

The Buddhist way of life has begun to appeal to many Westerners. Its search for peace of mind through meditation has made it increasingly popular. Its care for living creatures and the environment has also led many people to feel they can accept its teachings.

Buddhist worship in Kyoto, Japan.

Wesak

Known as Vesakha Puja, Vesak, Wesak or Buddha Day, this special festival happens on the full moon day in the Buddhist month of Vesakha, which usually occurs in the Western month of May.

It celebrates the birth, enlightenment and death of the Buddha.

At this time, his followers clean their homes and decorate them with flowers, lanterns and candles, visit their temples and offer gifts to the monks. They may release caged birds and 'bathe' or wash statues of the Buddha – in thanksgiving for his life and teachings.

It is a time when Buddhists think about the Five Precepts, how well they are living their lives and whether they are moving towards enlightenment.

Monks arrive at St Paul's Cathedral, London, for an interfaith service in remembrance of the victims of the tsunami disaster in 2005.

Bathing a small statue of the Buddha at Wesak.

Ahimsa

Because the laws of reincarnation, or samsara, mean that a person can be reborn as an animal or even an insect, Jains believe all forms of life have souls – and great care should be taken never to hurt even the smallest creature. This belief of 'not harming' is called 'ahimsa'.

When walking, some Jains wear face masks and will brush the ground with a light brush so that they neither swallow nor tread on any insect. Some Jain monks do not wash because washing might kill any parasites that are living on their bodies. Because of their belief in ahimsa, all Jains are vegetarians and try to live in such a way as to protect the world's resources.

A Svetambara monk (see opposite), wearing a face mask.

44 ✋ The Jains

The Jains do not believe in a god in the way that followers of other religions do. They believe there have been 24 'great souls', whom they call the *Tirthankaras*. They are regarded as teachers who have shown people the right way of living. Other religions might call the *Tirthankaras* 'prophets'. Little is known about their lives – except in the case of the twenty-fourth: a man called Mahavira. His name means 'great hero'.

Mahavira

Mahavira lived from 599 until 527 BCE – about the same time as the Buddha. Like the Buddha, he was born into a high caste family. At the age of 29, he decided to give up all his wealth and live as a wandering beggar.

After twelve years, he gathered twelve followers or disciples around him and began to share the wisdom he had learned. He spent the next 30 years teaching and preaching his messages of non-violence and the need to live harmlessly. He fasted so much that, in the end, he died of starvation.

The main teachings of Mahavira are called the 'Agamas'. Because Jain monks are allowed no possessions, these were memorized and passed on by word of mouth. Many were lost when a famine killed many Jain monks. The rest have since been written down.

Jain Beliefs

Jains do not pray to any god. They rely on teachers to help them learn to follow the right way of living – the aim of which is to break free from earthly life.

Jains believe in samsara: every human being has a soul that passes over from one life to another. The soul is made 'dirty' by bad karma, caused by bad deeds that one performs in a lifetime. Only when a person breaks free from karma can a soul gain true knowledge and freedom.

Worship

Because Jains do not worship gods, they do not go to their temples to 'please' a god or to ask for anything. Jains go to temples to help them concentrate (or meditate) on the ideal way of life. They may do this by meditating on one of the *Tirthankaras* and each temple will contain a statue or image of at least one of the *Tirthankaras*. During worship, Jains may repeat or chant mantras over and over again.

Jains also perform puja or worship before dawn in their own homes, pray before lunch and, at the end of the day, say sorry for any harm they have done that day.

Divisions

Over the years, Jains divided into two groups – mainly because of a disagreement about the teaching that monks should have no possessions. One group thought this meant that they should even give up all clothing and go 'sky-clad'. They are called the 'Digambaras' and follow Jain teaching very strictly. Even today, Digambara monks live completely naked. Digambaras also believe that women cannot reach moksha without being reborn as a man.

The other group, known as 'Svetambaras', believe monks should wear very simple white clothes.

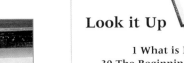

Look it Up

1 What is Religion?
30 The Beginnings of Hinduism
(Reincarnation)
34 Being a Hindu (Meditation)
38 The Prince and the Truth

A Way of Living

The three ideas that guide Jains in their daily lives are known as 'the Three Jewels':

- right belief
- right knowledge
- right conduct.

Jain monks, who spend much of their lives fasting, also make five vows or promises:

- never to use violence (ahimsa)
- never to steal
- always to be truthful
- never to have sexual relations
- have no unnecessary possessions.

Jains who are not monks 'do the best they can' to follow these five vows, which are known as *mahavratas*.

Sonagiri in the Indian state of Bhopal is a holy place for Digambara Jains. There are over a hundred temples in the area, all built of white stone.

Sikhism began in India, later than the other world faiths; its founder was Guru Nanak.

The Mool Mantra

There is only one God.

ਸਤਿ ਨਾਮੁ

Truth is his name.

ਕਰਤਾ ਪੁਰਖ

He is the creator.

ਨਿਰ ਭਉ

He is without fear.

ਨਿਰ ਵੈਰੁ

He is without hate.

ਅਕਾਲ ਮੂਰਤਿ

He is timeless and without form.

ਅਜੂਨੀ ਸੈਭੰ

He is beyond death, the enlightened one.

ਗੁਰ ਪ੍ਰਸਾਦਿ ॥

He can be known by the Guru's grace.

The Mool Mantra was the first poem or hymn written by Guru Nanak and it is written at the start of every chapter of the Sikh holy book, the Guru Granth Sahib. It sums up the main beliefs of the faith.

Look it Up

45 Guru Nanak

A little more than 500 years ago, there lived in a village called Talwandi a boy called Nanak. (Originally in India, Talwandi is now in Pakistan and is known as Nankana Sahib.) The boy was so intelligent that there came a time when his teachers said there was nothing left to teach him. When he grew up, he became the first leader or teacher of one of the great religions of the world, Sikhism.

Nanak was born into a Hindu family on 15 April 1469 CE. The people in that area were either Hindus or Muslims. Nanak saw good in both religions but did not like the Hindu caste system. Nor did he like some teachings of Islam. As he grew up, he was respected as a teacher, or 'guru'. He believed all men and women were equal. He taught that people should work hard and help others – and that there is only one God and that God is everywhere.

Guru Nanak, the founder of Sikhism.

Nanak's Visit to Makkah

Guru Nanak once made a journey to the Muslim holy city of Makkah. He was tired after his long journey so he lay down in the open air to rest. By chance, his feet were pointing towards the Muslim holy building, the Ka'bah. A Muslim teacher called Rukandin was nearby – and he, like all Muslims, faced Makkah and the Ka'bah whenever he said his prayers. He was horrified at what Nanak was doing.

'It's a great insult. You're pointing your dirty feet towards the holy house of God. It's most disrespectful.'

'I thought God was everywhere,' Nanak is said to have replied. 'Would you please turn me round so my feet are pointing in any direction where God is not present.'

Rukandin tried moving him round but Nanak stopped him. 'God doesn't live in one place. He is everywhere.'

Carrying on the Work

When Guru Nanak was about 50, he gave up his travels and started the building of a new town called Kartarpur in the area now known as the Punjab. He built a small shrine there and, in the evenings, all the townsfolk would gather there to listen to him.

They all cooked in the same kitchen and ate together, whether they were rich or poor.

One of his most faithful followers was a man known as Bhai Lahna. Guru Nanak gave him a new name, Angad, and said he would be the next Sikh Guru. A few days later, Guru Nanak died.

During his life, he wrote many poems for which a Muslim friend called Mardana played the music so they could be sung as hymns. Later, they became part of the Sikh holy book, the Guru Granth Sahib.

The Gurdwara Janam Asthan, which marks the birthplace of Guru Nanak in Nankana Sahib (Talwandi).

The festival of Hola Mohalla happens the day after Holi. It became a day for military training. It is now celebrated with displays of many skills.

Guru Nanak's Teachings

Guru Nanak's three main teachings are that his followers should meditate (*Naam japna*), earn an honest living (*Kirat karna*) and share what they have (*Vand chhakna*). His teachings are sometimes summarized this way:

1 There is only one God. Worship and pray to the one God and to no other.

2 Remember God, work hard and help others.

3 God is pleased with honest work and true living.

4 There is no rich, no poor, no black and no white before God. It is your actions that make you good or bad.

5 Men and women are all equal before God.

6 Love everyone and pray for the good of all.

7 Be kind to people, animals and birds.

8 Do not be afraid and do not frighten others.

9 Always speak the truth.

A Sikh farmer plants his field following the heavy monsoon rains in the Punjab region.

After Guru Nanak, there were nine more Sikh Gurus or teachers.

46 The Ten Gurus

Guru Gobind Singh created the Brotherhood of all Sikhs, which is known as the Khalsa. This Guru was the last of the great Sikh Gurus (in India, 'guru' can also be used of any respected teacher).

The Founding of the Khalsa

In the year 1699 CE, the tenth Sikh teacher and leader, Guru Gobind Singh, called all the Sikhs to meet him at a place called Anandpur at the festival of Baisakhi. 'By my sword,' said Guru Gobind Singh, 'I ask is there one among you who will prove his faith by giving me his head? Who will offer up his life?'

There was a long silence. Eventually, a warrior Sikh from Lahore stepped forward. 'My Guru and my lord. My humble head is yours, if so you wish it.' The Guru led him into the tent. From inside the tent, there came a dull thud. The Guru came out, his sword now dripping blood. 'If there be another true Sikh, let him now offer me his head as proof of his faith.'

This time a poor farmer from Delhi came forward. The Guru led him into the tent. Again a thud was heard. Again, the Guru reappeared with his sword dripping blood. Again he asked for the head of a Sikh. This time a washerman from Gujerat volunteered. He too was led into the tent; a thud was heard and the Guru reappeared with his sword now bloodier than ever. A fourth and fifth Sikh stepped forward when the Guru asked for yet more men to offer up their lives to prove their faith.

After the fifth Sikh had entered the tent and a fifth thud had been heard, there was a longer silence and then Guru Gobind Singh came out of his tent, not with his sword but followed by the five Sikhs who had offered up their lives. All were now dressed like the Guru in yellow robes tied with blue sashes and each was wearing a turban.

'These five have passed the test of faith,' said the Guru, 'and they shall be known as the Khalsa, the pure ones. They are soldier saints who will spread abroad the Sikh message of brotherhood and sisterhood.'

The five 'soldier saints' each came from a different caste – and since then Sikhism has been classless.

A painting showing Guru Nanak and the nine Gurus who became leaders of the faith after him.

Amrit

'Amrit' means 'nectar'.
It is a drink made from sugar and water, stirred with a sword. It was first prepared by Guru Gobind Singh and given to those who became the first five members of the Khalsa.
Sikhs continue to receive amrit when they join the Khalsa (see page 103).

Exactly 300 years after the founding of the Khalsa, the event is celebrated at the festival of Baisakhi in the streets of modern-day Anandpur.

The Ten Gurus

These are the years in which the ten Gurus (or spiritual leaders of the Sikhs) were born and died. After Guru Nanak, each became Guru on the death of the Guru before him.

Guru Nanak	1469–1539
Guru Angad	1504–1552
Guru Amar Das	1479–1574
Guru Ram Das	1534–1581
Guru Arjan Dev	1563–1606
Guru Hargobind	1595–1644
Guru Har Rai	1630–1661
Guru Har Krishan	1656–1664
Guru Tegh Bahadur	1621–1675
Guru Gobind Singh	1666–1708

Each Guru was chosen because he was thought to be the one who could best carry on Guru Nanak's work. It did not matter whether or not he was related to the Guru who came before him.

Each is remembered for something special. For example, Guru Angad chose the alphabet used to write down the language of the Sikhs, Punjabi. Until then, it was only a spoken language.

Sikhs in Delhi, India, remember the martyrdom of Guru Tegh Bahadur: the banner shows the Guru being asked to choose between being executed and becoming a Muslim.

The Martyrdom of Guru Tegh Bahadur

Because the Sikh religion began in a part of India ruled by Muslims, it was not always easy to be a Sikh. For example, in the days of the ninth Guru, Guru Tegh Bahadur, the Muslim Emperor of India, Aurangzeb, tried to make the Sikhs (and Hindus) Muslim.

Guru Tegh Bahadur decided to go and plead with Aurangzeb. His son, Gobind Rai, warned him he might be killed. Even so, Guru Tegh went to the emperor.

Emperor Aurangzeb would not listen and gave Guru Tegh Bahadur a choice: become a Muslim or die.

The Guru refused to give up his faith and was executed. Later, Gobind Rai was named as the next Guru and became known as Guru Gobind Singh. He taught a basic truth of Sikhism: all men and women should be equal: 'All people are the same, although they may look different. The fair-skinned and the dark; the Hindu, the Muslim… All human beings have the same eyes, the same ears, the same body. All human beings are reflections of the one God.'

Look it Up

34 Being a Hindu (The Caste System)
37 Hinduism in India – and Around the World (Ruled by Mughals)
45 Guru Nanak
47 The Guru Granth Sahib and the Gurdwara
49 Jorhmela and Gurpurbs

> Sikhs worship in buildings known as gurdwaras – in each of which is found a copy of their holy book.

47 ☬ The Guru Granth Sahib and the Gurdwara

When the tenth Sikh Guru, Guru Gobind Singh, founded the Khalsa, he said that there would be no more human gurus. Instead, from then on, Sikhs must turn to their holy book to hear God's teaching.

The Guru Granth Sahib

The Sikh holy book (or *granth*) is called the Guru Granth Sahib and is treated with great respect, as a living guru or teacher. The word *sahib* is an Indian word of respect meaning 'sir'.

It contains the teachings of the ten Gurus and also a large number of hymns. It is written in the script which Guru Angad developed – and many Sikhs learn to read this kind of writing so that they can read from their holy book.

If a family has their own copy, it is kept in a room of its own.

Inside a Gurdwara

A Sikh holy building is called a gurdwara. The word means 'doorway to the Guru': the gurdwara is the way or 'door' to the holy book, the Guru Granth Sahib.

Sikhs do not have a holy day in each week like some other religions. Worship takes place on whichever day is convenient – for example on Sundays in Western countries.

A gurdwara is not just a place of worship. It is also a social centre and a meeting place. There may be classrooms where young Sikhs are taught their faith. There will certainly be a kitchen (*langar*) where meals are prepared because Sikhs always eat together after the main service of the week. This is a sign of the brotherhood and sisterhood of all Sikhs – but anyone is welcome, whether they are Sikhs or not.

After worship in this gurdwara in Amritsar, Sikhs share a meal.

Sikh Worship

There are often separate entrances to the worship room for men and women. At each door are shoe racks because everyone entering a gurdwara removes their shoes. Everyone keeps their head covered. Both of these actions are signs of respect to the holy book.

The Guru Granth Sahib is kept in its own room until worship, or 'kirtan', begins. Then it is brought into the worship room where, at one end, there is a platform. Over the platform is a canopy called a *palki* or *chanani*. Under the canopy is a kind of throne. The Guru Granth Sahib is placed here. It is kept covered except when it is being read from.

The musician in the front of the picture is playing a tabla.

Behind the Guru Granth Sahib sits a person called the *granthi*. He or she is a person chosen or elected to read from the book. (Sikhs do not have priests.) The *granthi* may wave a special decorated fan (called a *chauri*) over the book while it is open and being read – a mark of its importance.

Besides listening to readings from the Guru Granth Sahib, the people sing hymns, led by musicians who are likely to play the 'tabla' (a small drum) and a small harmonium. Towards the end of worship (which may last several hours), the people stand to pray. This prayer is called the *Ardas,* during which Sikhs remember the ten Gurus and pray that they will be able to follow their teachings.

Everyone then shares the *karah parshad*. This is a kind of sweet food made from flour, butter, sugar and water. Everyone is given a small piece as a sign that, before God, all are equal.

After the service, a full meal is served in the *langar*.

The *granthi* leads worship in a gurdwara in Manchester, England.

The Guru Granth Sahib is read during worship in a gurdwara in London, England.

Reading the Guru Granth Sahib

At special festivals known as *gurpurbs*, the Guru Granth Sahib is read aloud from beginning to end. As the book contains 5,894 hymns and verses, this reading takes about 48 hours and is known as *Akhand Path*.

All copies of the Guru Granth Sahib are identical. It is always printed in the same way so that it has 1,430 pages.

Look it Up

48 ☬ The Golden Temple

The Sacred Pools

There has always been a pool at this place and it is considered holy by people of several faiths.

Hindus believe their god Rama was brought back to life after drinking its water.

Buddhists believe that their great teacher, the Buddha, once visited the pool.

Sikhs believe that their second Guru, Guru Angad, once had an illness that was cured by a herb that grew near the pool.

Just over 400 years ago, most of what is now India and Pakistan was ruled by a great Muslim leader called Emperor Akbar. He lived at the time of the fourth Sikh Guru, Guru Ram Das.

Guru Ram Das wanted to build a city where Sikhs could live and work together – and honour God. Emperor Akbar gave some land to the Sikhs so that they could build the city. Hundreds of Sikhs came to help. They built small huts in which to live and a *langar* where everyone ate together. At first it was just a small town and was named after the Guru: Ramdaspur.

When his son, Arjan Dev, became Guru, he carried on the work. There was already a pool or lake there and he had it made bigger and turned into two large pools, which were called 'Pools of Nectar', from which the city got its new name, Amritsar (*amrit* means 'nectar').

A temple was built in which Sikhs could worship God. That temple is now known as the Golden Temple because it is covered in gold. There are many carvings with hidden meanings on its walls. Some are of flowers and fruit, which remind Sikhs that life can be beautiful.

The temple has four entrances to show that all people are welcome – from whichever part of the world they come. The pool is now surrounded by many other holy buildings.

The Guru Granth Sahib is read continuously in the Golden Temple.

Sikhs gather around one of the 'Pools of Amrit' that surround the Golden Temple. The word *amrit* can also mean 'holy water'.

Crowds, including many pilgrims, celebrate outside the Golden Temple.

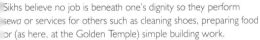

Sikhs believe no job is beneath one's dignity so they perform sewa or services for others such as cleaning shoes, preparing food or (as here, at the Golden Temple) simple building work.

Pilgrimage

Pilgrimage is not a duty for Sikhs. Some Sikhs feel the idea of making a pilgrimage is wrong or superstitious, as they believe God is present everywhere.

Even so, most Sikhs want to visit Amritsar during their life, as it is the centre of their faith. One reason they want to do this is because the temple contains some of the earliest handwritten copies ever made of the Guru Granth Sahib.

When they do visit, they bathe in the pool, cross the causeway to the temple, take off their shoes and then enter the temple. Inside, they walk respectfully past the Guru Granth Sahib.

Every 50 years, thousands of Sikhs come to Amritsar to help clean the pools. This type of help is called *sewa,* or service. Sikhs believe *sewa* is a way of honouring God. Many do *sewa* at home or in their local gurdwara – or by helping sick or poor people.

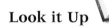

Look it Up

Sikhs celebrate events in the lives of the Gurus and have also adapted some Hindu festivals.

Martyrdom of Guru Arjan Dev

The martyrdom of the fifth of the ten Sikh Gurus (or teachers) in 1606 CE is observed worldwide by members of the faith.

The man who was emperor of India at that time, Emperor Jahangir, became jealous of Guru Arjan and accused him of helping his brother and rival. Arjan was brought before Jahangir and ordered to pay a huge fine and to alter the words of the holy book. Arjan refused – even though he knew this would result in death. It did. He was forced to sit in a red-hot cauldron over a fire and boiling water was poured on him until he died.

In his memory, Sikhs hold processions and give out sherbet or drinks of fruit juice, inviting passers-by to be refreshed 'in the Guru's name'.

49 ☬ Jorhmela and Gurpurbs

Three important Sikh celebrations happen at about the same time as the Hindu spring festival called Baisakhi and as the holy days of Divali and Holi. These festivals or fairs are known as *jorhmela*.

Jorhmela

It was Guru Amar Das who said that Sikhs should gather together for worship at Baisakhi and Divali. This meant that, in the early days of the Sikh faith, people had to decide whether to go to a Hindu or a Sikh celebration – which meant they had to decide whether they were Hindus or Sikhs.

Baisakhi is celebrated in April as a time of thanksgiving when the harvest is gathered in. Guru Gobind Singh gave the festival a new meaning in 1699 CE when he founded the Khalsa. In memory of this, Sikhs who want to join the Khalsa often do so at Baisakhi.

Divali happens in October or November. For Hindus, it is a festival of light. For Sikhs it is a reminder of how Guru Hargobind was once put in prison – and then pardoned. He refused to leave the prison until a number of Hindus were also set free.

Sikhs celebrate Hola Mohalla the day after Holi. It was established by Guru Gobind Singh as a day for military training so that Sikhs were ready to defend their faith.

Nihang (traditional religious warriors) ride in procession at an annual Hola Mohalla celebration at Anandpur Sahib in the Punjab region of northern India.

Sikhs walk in procession alongside the holy Guru Granth Sahib to mark Guru Nanak's birthday.

Guru Nanak's Birthday

A government tax collector called Kalu was anxiously waiting for his wife Tripta to give birth. Suddenly, the nurse ran out to give the good news to Kalu. 'Congratulations. Your wife has given birth to a fine boy.'

'But I haven't heard a baby crying,' said Kalu.

'That was the strange thing,' said the nurse. 'Instead of crying, the baby smiled as he was born. I think he will be very special.' The baby was named Nanak, meaning 'the special one'.

Sikhs mark his birthday with a non-stop reading of the Guru Granth Sahib (*Akhand Path*) in their gurdwaras. People stay as long as possible, returning after work or looking after children. During this time, food is prepared in the *langar* for the readers and worshippers. In many places, on the actual birthday the holy book is carried on a platform under a canopy in a procession through the streets. Everyone then returns to their homes for a special meal together.

Gurpurbs

Those Sikh festivals which celebrate events in the lives of the Gurus are known as *gurpurbs*. The three most important are the birthday of Guru Nanak, the birthday of Guru Gobind Singh and the day when Guru Arjan was put to death. Since the introduction of the new Sikh calendar (see right), these festivals are now celebrated on the same date on that calendar each year. *Jorhmela* still have their dates set by the Hindu calendar.

In many gurdwaras, the yellow and white Sikh flag is taken down and carefully washed at the festival of Baisakhi.

Look it Up

35 Hindu Festivals
45 Guru Nanak
46 The Ten Gurus
47 The Guru Granth Sahib
and the Gurdwara

The Sikh Calendar

Sikhs originally used the Hindu calendar. In 2003, over 300 years after the founding of the Khalsa, a new calendar was introduced. The years of this calendar (the *Nanakshahi* calendar) are counted from the birth of Guru Nanak in 1469.

This list of *jorhmela* and some of the *gurpurbs* shows the Western months in which they happen.

December/January: Birthday of Guru Gobind Singh

February/March: Hola Mohalla

April: Baisakhi

June: Martyrdom of Guru Arjan

October/November: Divali

October/November: Birthday of Guru Nanak

November/December: Martyrdom of Guru Tegh Bahadur

There are five symbols that show membership of the Khalsa.

50  The Five Ks

When Guru Gobind Singh founded the Khalsa, he said that Sikhs should show their membership in special ways. Because the Punjabi word for each of these five ways begins with the letter K, they are known as the Five Ks.

Kesh

Kesh is uncut hair. In Sikhism, the human body is said to be holy or sacred because it contains the living spirit of that person. As hair is an essential part of that body, the hair must never be cut or thrown away. For this reason, Sikhs wear their hair long. Men also wear their beards and moustaches long.

The uncut hair of a Sikh is a sign of his or her promise to live his or her whole life for God. The hair must be kept tidy, washed at least every four days and never dyed.

The Turban

Although many people recognize Sikh men by their turban, it is not one of the symbols of the faith. It is worn by Sikh men as a way of keeping their long hair clean and tidy. Guru Gobind Singh wore a turban and Sikhs also wear turbans to be like the Guru. The most popular colours are blue, yellow or black.

Younger boys, whose hair has not grown as long, wear a small handkerchief (called a *rumal*) to tie up their hair.

Kangha

The kangha is a small comb worn to keep the hair in place. Brushed or tidy hair is thought to be a sign of discipline and cleanliness.

Kangha

Kesh

Those Sikhs who join the Khalsa follow the instruction by Guru Gobind Singh to wear the Five Ks, knowing every member of the Khalsa has done so since 1699 CE.

Kirpan

Kachera (or kaccha)

Kara

A Sikh soldier, wearing a turban, carries a young boy (also wearing an adult man's turban) in a religious procession.

Look it Up

Kirpan

The kirpan is a sword worn by Sikhs to remind them that they are fighters for God and justice. It is not a weapon for attacking people but for defending the Sikh faith and for protecting the weak and helpless.

Nowadays, Sikhs wear only a miniature kirpan – or even a very tiny one set in the kangha.

Kachera (or kaccha)

At the time of Guru Gobind Singh, many Indian men wore only a loose loin cloth called a 'dhoti'. The kachera are shorts worn by both men and women to be respectable at all times and to allow easy movement when working or in battle.

Kara

The kara is a circular steel bracelet, worn on the right wrist by men and women. It is a sign that God is one, with no beginning and no end. It is made of steel and is a reminder to be strong.

A Sikh husband and wife prepare a family meal.

Growing Up as a Sikh

When a Sikh baby is born, the Sikh holy book, the Guru Granth Sahib, is opened at any page. The first letter of the first hymn (or other writing) at the top of the left hand page will be the first letter of the baby's first name. If the baby is a boy he will also be given the name 'Singh' (meaning 'lion'). If she is a girl, she will also be called 'Kaur' (princess).

In Sikhism, entry into full membership of the faith (the Khalsa) happens with a special ceremony.

It takes place in a gurdwara and is led by five adult Sikhs who wear special yellow robes. Before it starts, each young person makes a vow that he or she will dedicate him or herself to the way of life taught by the ten Gurus. Prayers are said and a hymn is sung.

Then the five Sikhs stir sugar into a bowl of water, using a sword. This holy water is called 'amrit'. A small amount is poured into each young person's hands and some is sprinkled on their eyes as a sign that they should see no evil. Then a little amrit is placed on their head. In this way, the most important parts of the body are made holy.

When Sikhs live outside India, they believe it is especially important for children to learn about the traditions of their faith. Sikh children learn these at the gurdwara and from their parents and grandparents.

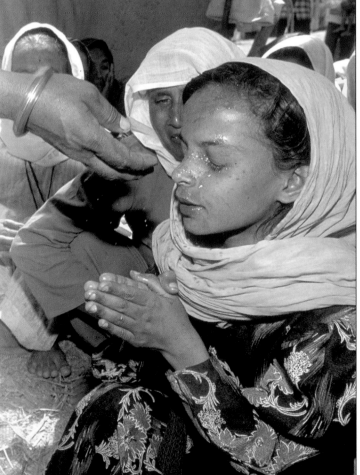

Some Sikhs become members of the Khalsa at quite a young age. Here, a group receive amrit at their ceremony.

Chinese religion is made up of a number of different beliefs.

51 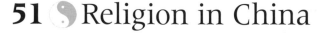Religion in China

Many Chinese people do not choose to belong to one religion. They feel able to follow those teachings from various Chinese religions which they find helpful. They celebrate family events and festivals according to these different traditions.

The Chinese Calendar

The Chinese calendar is the oldest in the world, dating from 2500 BCE. Long after it was created, the founder of Buddhism, known as the Buddha, lived in India. Near the time of his death, it is said he asked all the animals to visit him. Twelve came: the rat, ox, tiger, rabbit, dragon, snake, horse, sheep, monkey, cock, dog and boar (or pig) – and he named the years in that order.

When Buddhism reached China, the Chinese came to believe that the animal ruling the year in which you are born is an influence on your personality, saying: 'This is the animal that hides in your heart.'

In the Chinese calendar, each year is named after one of these twelve animals.

The Three Ways
The three most important religious traditions in China are:

- Confucianism
- Taoism (sometimes written Daoism)
- Buddhism.

Confucianism and Taoism developed in China. Buddhism reached China in the first century CE. It began to influence many parts of Chinese life (such as the naming of each year after an animal).

Popular Religion
Besides these three religions, a much older 'religion of the people' (or popular religion) has survived. It is sometimes called a 'folk religion' or 'village religion'.

In ancient times, people depended on the sun, wind and rain to grow the crops that gave them food. In China, they asked the spirits that they believed controlled these elements for the weather they needed – and gave them thanks when it arrived.

The people also believed that other spirits or gods brought peace and happiness (or 'harmony') to each home. These 'ancient' gods are still honoured at such times as family birthdays and New Year.

Popular religion in China taught that it was important that everything should be in balance. This created the idea of 'yin' and 'yang'.

Many Chinese believe there is peace and harmony in a family or in the world when two forces known as 'yin' and 'yang' are in balance. 'Yin' stands for all that is cool, soft, dark and female. 'Yang' stands for everything that is hot, hard, light and male. This symbol shows yin and yang in balance.

Look it Up

Communism

In 1949, the Communist Party came to power in China. Its leader was a man called Mao Zedong (sometimes spelled Tse-tung). He tried to stop people believing in all religions.

Later, in 1966, the Communists tried again to get rid of what they thought were old-fashioned, wrong beliefs. This was known as the Cultural Revolution. For example, the teachings of Confucius were said to be wrong or even rubbish.

Even so, many people held true to their religious beliefs. Because of this, it was agreed that some religious groups could become 'official'. That is, people could follow their religions provided the Communists checked what they were doing and saying. To avoid this interference, some people followed their religion in secret.

In more recent times, there has been greater religious freedom.

Mao Zedong, who was president of China from 1949 until 1959 but who remained chairman of its Communist Party until his death in 1976.

Chinese New Year

Long ago in one part of China, there lived a ferocious monster called Nian. Whenever food was scarce in midwinter, Nian would leave the forests and lumber into the nearest village in the hope of finding someone to catch – and eat. Nobody knew how to frighten Nian away. Then, one day, a villager happened to hang a bright red sheet from a tree. Frightened by the brightness of the sheet, Nian turned, ran away and was never seen again.

At New Year, in memory of this legend, Chinese people stick sheets of red paper to their doors, gates and houses to protect them from evil. They also cut gold paper into the shape of words, saying such things as 'May we be happy for ever' and stick these sayings on the red banners.

Before the new year starts, houses are spring-cleaned to get rid of all past misfortunes. At 11pm on the night of the new moon, joss sticks are lit and fireworks set off to scare away all evil. Next day (New Year's Day), everyone eats dumplings made from sticky rice or flour. In one will be hidden a piece of gold or silver or a jewel. Whoever finds it will have good luck for the whole year.

In China, dragons are said to bring good luck, and New Year is celebrated with 'dragon dances' – in which dancers inside a 'dragon' make it sway and twirl through the streets.

The Chinese religion Confucianism is concerned mainly with the way people behave towards one another.

Tian

Confucius was mainly concerned about how people behaved on earth but he also believed that if people led good lives, then they would find peace and harmony in heaven – known in China as *Tian*.

Heaven means to be one with God.

Confucius: Analects

52 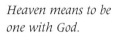Confucianism

Confucians follow the teachings of K'ung Fu-tzu or Confucius. He believed in showing kindness to one another and respect to parents and the elderly – and in spreading harmony between people.

The Story of K'ung Fu-tzu

K'ung Fu-tzu worked for the government of the region where he lived, which was called Lu. He planned the building of new roads and bridges, started schools and established a fair system of justice. Eventually, he was made a special adviser to its ruler, Duke Ai.

One day, Duke Ai asked him, 'What else must I do to make the people respect me?'

'If you promote good people over the bad, you'll be respected. If you let the bad take advantage of the good, then you won't be respected.' He also pointed out that the poor people had to work hard to pay for the extravagance of the wealthy. Saying this made K'ung Fu-tzu unpopular – so he left the region. A few students journeyed with him, in a small procession of simple carriages.

Eventually they came to a part of the country called Wei, which was ruled by Duke Ling. Here, K'ung Fu-tzu started teaching.

The Life of K'ung Fu-tzu

Little is known for certain about K'ung Fu-tzu, who lived from 551 to 479 BCE. At about the age of 50, he became a well-known travelling teacher and his sayings spread throughout China. When Westerners first heard about him they translated his name into Latin as 'Confucius'.

Some people say he was tall and very dignified. Others say he had big ears and sticking-out front teeth. Some suggest he was a fussy, niggling, old-fashioned sort of person. From his sayings (which were written down by his disciples), we know he was kind and generous; he liked making jokes, swimming and playing other sports.

An ancient painting of K'ung Fu-tzu.

This painting shows a Chinese emperor with his soldiers and courtiers.

Duke Ling of Wei had been wanting to attack a neighbouring city and, knowing K'ung Fu-tzu was wise, asked him the best way of leading an attack. Not wishing to become involved in war, K'ung Fu-tzu and his friends again moved on, now in disguise.

In one village, they met a woman who was crying bitterly. She told K'ung Fu-tzu how her husband, uncle and son had all been killed by a tiger. 'Why don't you move away, to a safe district?' he asked.

'But here we have a good ruler,' she answered. 'I wouldn't move to where there's a bad government.'

'You see,' said K'ung Fu-tzu to his students, 'bad government is worse than a tiger.'

Soon after this, men brought presents from Duke Ai of Lu, who had realized how wise K'ung Fu-tzu was and wanted him to return. K'ung Fu-tzu agreed and they returned to Lu, where his disciples wrote down his sayings.

One disciple, Tseng Tzu, wrote down what he had learned about how to be a good learner or student:

'Every night, I ask myself three things. In what I have done for others today, have I done my best? To my friends, have I been loyal and true? And have I told others to do only what I would do myself?'

Look it Up

51 Religion in China

Teachings of K'ung Fu-tzu

The main teaching of K'ung Fu-tzu is this:

Do not do to others what you do not wish to be done to you.

Among his many other sayings are:

Don't eat food that hasn't been properly prepared or which has gone bad.

Don't eat except at meal times. Eat wisely, eat slowly.

Never mind when people are rude to you. That is the wise way.

Confucianism also teaches people to respect learning and to study and to work hard. Even after China became Communist, these Confucian teachings survived.

53 🌀 Taoism

Lao-tzu

The founder or first teacher of Taoism is said to have been a poet and wise man called Lao-tzu, who lived in the sixth century BCE. He is often described as the author of one of the two important Taoist collections of writings, the Tao-Te-Ching. One story about him retells how he was once travelling on an ox and came to a frontier. There he was asked to write down all that he thought was important.

The word 'Taoism' is pronounced 'dow-ism'. Because of this, it is sometimes written Daoism.

This statue of Lao-tzu is near the city of Quanzhou in south-east China.

The result was the Tao-Te-Ching. He then disappeared – becoming part of the Tao.

Nowadays, many people think that Lao-tzu was not a real person and that the book Tao-Te-Ching was written by a number of wise old people of that time.

Followers of Taoism follow 'the Tao'. The Tao is not God. The Tao is not worshipped. There are many Tao gods and goddesses that look after different parts of life (such as long life, happiness and wealth). They are worshipped in Taoist temples. But like all created things, these gods and goddesses are part of the Tao.

The Tao is not just a way of life but also the force or power that created the universe.

A Taoist nun sweeps the steps of the Beichan Temple (which has also been a Buddhist temple) in Xining in north-east China.

The Tao-Te-Ching and another famous Taoist collection of writings, the Chuang Tzu, both teach that it is important to keep the forces of yin and yang in balance, and to accept both good luck and bad luck with equal happiness. If a person follows the Tao, it is believed that person will have long life followed by everlasting life.

If the forces of yin and yang are not in balance, the result may be disease.

Taoists believe that the human body is a network of invisible channels (known as meridians) through which energy can flow to nourish the body. If very fine needles are put into the flesh at the correct crossing points of these channels, harmony between yin and yang is restored and an illness is cured.

This method of treatment is now known in the West as acupuncture.

Look it Up

Taoism and Communism

After the Communist takeover of China, Taoism was banned. Within ten years, the number of its followers is believed to have fallen by 99 per cent. Taoism then began to flourish in Taiwan, which had once been part of China.

When the Cultural Revolution came to an end in China and the new government allowed greater religious freedom, Taoism revived. There are now many Taoist temples throughout the country.

A Taoist nun prepares an altar table before a ceremony in the ancient Qingyanggong (or Green Goat) Temple in Chengdu, Sichuan, China.

Lantern Festival

There are many legends and beliefs about the Chinese Lantern Festival. One story tells how, thousands of years ago, in a small Chinese town, a man killed a goose. What the man didn't know was that this was the favourite goose of Emperor Yu-huang.

The emperor was so angry the goose had been killed that he decided to destroy the entire town by fire. However, a good spirit warned the man what was going to happen. He persuaded his friends to hang hundreds of lanterns throughout the town so that it would look as if it was already on fire.

Seeing the blazing lights, the emperor believed the town had already been punished for killing the goose. Ever since, Chinese people have celebrated for three nights at the time of the first full moon after the Chinese New Year. They parade paper lanterns of different shapes and colours through the streets, stage dragon dances and light fireworks.

The festival has changed little over the last 2,000 years except that now the processions may include elaborately lit floats and other exotic electric illuminations. In some places in northern China, blocks of ice are carved into the shape of human beings and burning candles are placed in holes inside them so they look like cold, white ghosts.

Many Chinese believe the Lantern Festival also celebrates the birthday of the Taoist god of fortune, Tianguan. Others say it is a Buddhist festival celebrating the arrival of Buddhism from India.

54 ⛩ Shinto

Long, long ago, according to Japanese legends, the powers (or gods) that controlled the winds and rain and thunder came to live on earth, making their homes in certain rivers, mountains, trees, oceans and other natural features.

These beings or spirits became known as 'kami' and, over time, each came to have shrines, or *jinja,* where people came to honour the spirit. One of the most famous shrines in Japan is Mount Fuji, which used to be a volcano. It is visited by many pilgrims. Anything that harms these places is thought to be an attack on the kami.

Over the centuries, many ideas from Confucianism reached Japan and became mixed with Shinto beliefs. When Buddhism reached Japan, it too became part of Japanese religion and people began to think of the kami as Buddhas.

A torii gate, the symbol of Shinto, built in a Japanese lake close to a Shinto shrine.

Facts about Shinto

• The word *Shinto* comes from the Chinese *shin tao* which is a translation of the Japanese *kami-no-michi.* It means 'way of the gods'.
• Shinto has no founder or creator.
• Shinto has no holy book.
• Shinto has no agreed set of beliefs or creed.
• Followers of Shinto honour the ancestors of the family, especially at the festival of Higan, which happens twice a year (in spring and autumn) when the day and night are of equal length. It is a time for visiting family graves. In spring in southern Japan, Higan happens when the cherry trees are in blossom – and people picnic under the trees.

Creation

Although there is no Shinto 'holy book', there are two very important books of myths. They are the Kojiki and the Nihonshoki. They were written in the eighth century CE and contain stories telling how the world was created.

Before the kami came to earth, there were seven generations of gods. The last of these were a brother and sister, Izanagi and Izanami. Their job was to 'complete and solidify the drifting land'. Izanagi dipped a jewelled spear into the sea, lifted it out and let drops of sea-water fall from it. These became the islands of Japan. Then, Izanagi and Izanami created the kami.

Izanagi dipping a jewelled spear into the sea.

Friends and families mark *Higan* with a picnic under cherry trees.

Look it Up

Shinto Worship

In Shinto, worship involves attending or serving the kami. Worship may be private or public.

When performed at a shrine, worshippers wash their hands and rinse their mouths before entering. As they enter the prayer hall, or *haiden*, they announce their arrival by clapping their hands twice. They may make a gift of money, ring a bell and bow to the kami of that shrine. Then they offer their prayers.

Pregnant women visit shrines to ask for the safe birth of their child. When a boy is born, the baby is carried to the shrine for a blessing 32 days after the birth. In the case of a girl, the baby is brought after 33 days. Later, at the ages of three, five or seven, children are brought to the shrine so that evil or danger may not harm them in the future.

Many Japanese people feel very close to the kami and believe the kami know their needs.

Children worship at a shrine in Kyoto, Japan.

Mount Fuji.

In Modern Times

During the 1800s, there was a wish to make Shinto 'pure'. In 1868 CE, all signs of Buddhism were taken out of Shinto shrines. Schools began to teach the ways of Shinto and to teach that the emperor of Japan and his family were related to the kami. Complete obedience to the emperor was now expected from everyone.

In 1946, after Japan had been defeated in the Second World War, the emperor of Japan at that time, Hirohito, announced that he was not in fact a god. From then on, Shinto was no longer the state religion and had no place in state schools.

Worship is now very much a personal affair but it is still very important in many Japanese people's lives, and Shinto ideas are again often mixed with Buddhist ones. It is quite common for a Japanese family to celebrate the birth of a baby or a marriage with Shinto ceremonies – and for the same family to use Buddhist ones at the time of a death.

New religious groups continue to develop, some growing out of the Christian faith.

55 † New Christian Groups

Sects and Cults

Many of the great religions can be said to have started as a small group, sect or cult. Many of them began with one leader who, at first, attracted a small group of followers, out of whom has grown a worldwide faith.

New religious groups still come into being, often being known as sects or cults.

The word 'sect' is generally used to mean a group that breaks away from an existing religion. The word 'cult' usually means a brand new religious faith with its own new rules and customs.

Occasionally a new sect or cult can be dangerous – either because it is very secretive (unlike those religions which preach openly) or because it uses tricks to persuade young people to join and then makes it difficult for them to leave.

Religions change. Over the years, they develop new understandings. For example, Christians once believed it was not wrong to own slaves (because slavery was common in biblical times). Nowadays, Christianity teaches slavery is wrong because God is described in the Bible as the one who sets slaves free.

Sometimes, a group of Christians have felt things were going wrong in their Church and have left to start new ones. Some of these 'new' Churches are now accepted as part of the worldwide Christian family.

Church of Jesus Christ of Latter-day Saints

This is often known as the Mormon Church. It was started by a man called Joseph Smith in the United States of America, who lived from 1805 to 1844. When he was 14, he went for a walk in some woods and believed he met both God and Jesus, who told him not to join any Christian Church.

When he was 18, an angel whom he called Moroni appeared to him and told him there was a book written on pages of gold hidden on a nearby hill. Four years later, Joseph found it. It was written in Hebrew and he translated it into English. It told a story of how Israelites had journeyed to South America 4,000 years earlier and how Jesus visited them after his resurrection. The leader of these people, Mormon, was killed in battle but gave the book to his son to keep safe.

Joseph Smith began preaching and gathering followers. Some people opposed him and he was eventually killed. A man called Brigham Young took his place and the Mormons moved to live near the Great Salt Lake in what is now the state of Utah.

The Mormon place of worship, known as the Tabernacle, in Salt Lake City, Utah.

Joseph Smith, founder of the Church of Jesus Christ of Latter-day Saints.

All Mormons are called 'saints'. They are baptized by immersion when they are eight. When they grow up, they are usually expected to spend two years (men) or 18 months (women) persuading other people to become Mormons.

Mormons say Joseph Smith was a great prophet but they worship God, Jesus and the Holy Spirit. They believe it is their job to make the world ready for the return of Jesus. They never drink alcohol, tea or coffee but no longer hold the belief (which they once did) that a man can have several wives.

Those who join the church as adults are baptized in the same way as Mormon children.

Jehovah's Witnesses

This sect began in the United States of America in 1872. It was started by a businessman named Charles Taze Russell. He had become unhappy with the Christian church of which he was a member. After reading the writings of a Baptist leader who believed there were many secret, hidden meanings in the Bible, he became convinced the world would end in 1873 or 1874.

When this did not happen, he decided Jesus was alive in the world but only 144,000 people who became 'Jehovah's Witnesses' would see him and be saved when the world did come to an end. He decided this would, after all, be in 1881, later changing the date to 1914 then to 1925 when it failed to happen.

When it did not end in 1925, his followers changed the date to 1975. A million people gave up being Jehovah's Witnesses when 1975 came and nothing happened. Even so, the movement is still strong.

Jehovah's Witnesses see the Bible as the main way in which God tells humans how they should behave. Jehovah's Witnesses do not believe in the Trinity but say that Jesus is a lesser being than God.

Seventh Day Adventists

Like Jehovah's Witnesses, Seventh Day Adventists believe the Second Coming of Jesus may happen any time soon. They also keep Saturday as a day of rest (as do the Jews) and not Sunday (as Christians do).

Unlike Jehovah's Witnesses, Seventh Day Adventists believe in the Trinity and the teachings of the Bible.

A minister leads Seventh Day Adventist Saturday worship.

Look it Up

16 'I Believe...'
58 Faith Around the World Today

From its beginnings in
Persia (now Iran), the
aim of the Bahá'í Faith
is the unity of all
peoples and
all faiths.

Being a Bahá'í

- Bahá'ís say daily prayers but have no priests.
- Bahá'ís do not drink or take drugs.
- Bahá'ís undergo a period of fasting every year.
- Bahá'ís believe marriage is important and encourage it.
- Bahá'ís may marry someone who is not a follower of the religion.
- Bahá'ís feel that divorce should be discouraged.
- Bahá'ís never use armed force in their own defence, nor do they maintain any armies.
- When people become Bahá'ís, they do not have to deny their original religion.
- Bahá'ís believe in equal rights for all people.

Abdu'l Bahá, son of Bahá'u'lláh.

Look it Up

56 ☼ The Bahá'í Faith

It all began one May day in the year 1844 CE in what was then called Persia and is now Iran. A young merchant called Siyyid Ali-Muhammad began to preach that a new world of peace and justice was at hand. He gave himself the title of Báb, an Arabic word which means 'gate'. He said that he was preparing the way for a prophet far greater than himself.

The Báb had been a Muslim and, at first, continued to follow the Muslim faith. In his teaching, he longed for a new prophet to appear. This offended the Shi'ah Muslims of Persia and, as his teaching spread, the shah, or ruler, of Persia began to fear a revolution. He put the Báb in prison. In 1850 he was taken before a firing squad. When the smoke of the shots cleared, the Báb was nowhere to be seen. He was found back in his cell, unharmed and teaching a disciple. When he had finished, he told the guards to do their duty. This time he really was killed.

The Founder, Bahá'u'lláh

In the two years following the Báb's death, there were more conflicts involving his followers, some of whom were put in prison on various charges. One of those imprisoned was a man named Mirza Husayn Ali Nuri, who later became known as Bahá'u'lláh. On his release, he had all his wealth taken away from him, was exiled from Persia and journeyed on foot to Baghdad in what is now Iraq. In 1863, he announced that he was the prophet the Báb had promised and he became the leader of the religion now known as the Bahá'í Faith.

In the year 1868, Bahá'u'lláh created the Bahá'í greeting, *Allah-u-Abha* ('God is all-glorious'), and from then on his followers began to be known as Bahá'ís.

Bahá'u'lláh died in the year 1892 and his son Abdu'l Bahá became leader. In the early years of the twentieth century, he journeyed to Britain and the United States of America. Bahá'í groups came into being in the places he visited. He spent the last eight years of his life in what is now Israel, working for peace in that land.

In recent years, the religion has again been persecuted in Iran but in other countries the faith has grown rapidly.

The Barli Development Centre in Indore, India, was started by Bahá'ís to teach women from rural areas new skills that will improve life for them, their families and their communities.

Haifa

Bahá'u'lláh visited the town of Haifa (in what is now Israel) four times in the later years of his life. He showed his son Abdu'l Bahá where the Báb's body should be laid to rest on the rocky hillside of Mount Carmel. The shrine there is now a place where Bahá'ís go on pilgrimage.

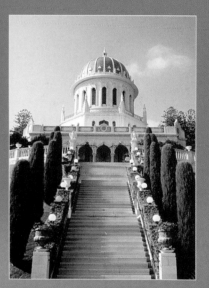

The Bahá'í Shrine on Mount Carmel, Israel.

Bahá'í Teachings

Bahá'u'lláh taught: 'The earth is but one country and all mankind its citizens.' For this reason, Bahá'ís hope and work for world peace, believing in the equality of men and women and the oneness of the human race. If a family does not have enough money to educate all its children, it should educate the girls – because they will be mothers and will educate the next generation.

Bahá'ís also believe in the importance of caring for the planet's natural resources and for those in need. They also work for an end to prejudice and the elimination of extreme wealth and poverty.

Bahá'u'lláh wanted to bring peace to the world and to unite all races. He believed all religions are like chapters in one book and that their leaders (including Krishna, the Buddha, Moses, Jesus and Muhammad) are all equal, like the rays from the sun. Bahá'ís believe that God will send more such prophets in the future.

The Bahá'í house of worship in New Delhi, India.

57 🌳 New Religious Movements

During the 1970s, many young people in Western countries became interested in Eastern religions. This happened partly because people were attracted to a simple way of life and felt dissatisfied with Western ways. Two movements in particular became popular in Europe and North America.

Rastafarians

The first Rastafarians were Jamaicans. Inspired by a politician called Marcus Garvey, Rastafarians or 'Rastas' came to believe that Haile Selassie, who was crowned emperor of Ethiopia (in East Africa) in 1930 CE, was a living God and that Ethiopia is their 'promised land'.

These beliefs are based on the idea that black people are descended from God's 'chosen people'. Rastas believe that when the Jews were forced out of their 'Promised Land' by the Romans in 70 CE, some moved into Ethiopia. The Ethiopians became God's 'chosen people' – later to be taken as slaves from Africa to Jamaica.

A Rastafarian shopkeeper in Jamaica.

Rastafarians (or Rastas) do not cut their hair but wear it in 'dreadlocks'. Men often wear hats made in 'Rasta' colours: red for the blood of the slaves from whom they are descended, gold for the wealth of Ethiopia and green for nature.

They eat only 'i-tal' food (food that is 'clean'). This means that (like Jews) they do not eat pork or shellfish. More strictly, they do not drink milk, coffee or rum or use salt. Nor do they smoke tobacco.

The Unification Church

This religious movement began in 1954 CE. It mixes Christian and Taoist teachings and was started by a man known as the Reverend Sun Myung Moon. Because of this, its followers are sometimes known as 'Moonies', although they do not like this name.

Sun Myung Moon was born in 1920 in North Korea. When he was 16, he had a vision in which he saw Jesus. He became an engineer in Japan and studied the Bible in great detail and developed teachings which became known as the 'Divine Principle'. This book is now the holy book of members of the Unification Church.

Sun Myung Moon returned to North Korea to start teaching his message but was put in prison. After three years, he was set free and walked to South Korea, carrying another ex-prisoner on his back. In 1954, he started his Unification Church. Its members see their aim as being the creation of a moral society based on the family. For this reason, marriage is very important to them and the Church sometimes holds mass weddings.

Sun Myung Moon conducts the wedding of a large number of Unification Church members.

Hare Krishna

The Hare Krishna movement (also known as the International Society for Krishna Consciousness) grew out of Hinduism. It was started by a man called Swami Prabhupada. The word 'swami' is a title given to respected teachers. He wanted to tell people in the West that they should 'wake up', realize what is truly important about life and not worry about money or possessions.

He taught that one way to do this is to chant a 'mantra' containing two of the names of the Hindu gods:

Hare Krishna, Hare Krishna,
Krishna, Krishna, Hare, Hare
Hare Rama, Hare Rama,
Rama, Rama, Hare, Hare.

As soon as the Swami first spoke in New York, USA, in 1965, the movement gained in popularity in the West. Like Hindus, its followers believe in samsara and hope for moksha. They also believe it is important to learn the Hindu scriptures, especially the Bhagavad Gita.

A Hare Krishna temple in Kerala, in southern India.

Modern-day Druids celebrate Samhain, a festival marking the start of winter, at the ancient Stonehenge monument in Wiltshire, England.

Look it Up

7 The Promised Land
30 The Beginnings of Hinduism (Reincarnation)
31 One God or Many Gods
32 Hindu Holy Writings
53 Taoism

Paganism

The word 'pagan' comes from a Latin word meaning 'peasant' or 'country dweller'. In recent years, a number of people (mainly white people living in Europe or North America – and especially ones who have grown up in towns and cities) have been trying to find ways of living closer to nature.

Some of these people have returned to the beliefs of the nature religions that existed in Europe before Christianity. Their beliefs are sometimes called 'New Paganism' or 'Neo-Paganism'.

Neo-Pagans do not worship the devil or kill or harm animals as is sometimes said. Instead, they may worship the sun, rivers, trees and changing seasons. Most Neo-Pagans respect the environment and want to avoid damaging it. Pagans also believe men and women are equal.

They often observe ancient festivals such as Beltane (the start of summer on 1 May), Lammas (the end of summer and start of harvest on 1 August) and Samhain (31 October). In particular, they mark sunrise on Midsummer Day just as ancient pagans known as Druids did, in circles of huge stones like Stonehenge in southern England.

Despite changes in modern life, faith remains important to most people in the world.

Sacred and Secular

The word 'secular' is the opposite of the words 'sacred' and 'holy'. It means 'not to do with religion' or 'concerned with worldly things'.

Secular countries do not have an official religion, nor do they teach a particular religion in schools. The United States of America is a secular country. Its laws, or Constitution, states that 'Congress shall make no law respecting an establishment of religion'. It also says people should be free to follow a religion of their choice.

Another secular country is Turkey. However, most people in Turkey are Muslim and Turks are divided as to whether Islam should become the 'official' religion of that country. In other Muslim countries, there are debates whether they should introduce Islamic law known as 'Shar'ia' (or sacred) law.

In modern times, more and more people have asked questions such as, 'Do we still need religions?'

Look it Up

58 🌳 Faith Around the World Today

In recent years, followers of many religions have left their homelands. For example, Hinduism has become a world faith not by seeking new members but because Hindus have left India in search of work. The same is true of Sikhism. Two faiths (Christianity and Islam) are spreading because they seek new members or converts.

Christianity

More than one third of the world's population now describe themselves as Christian. It is the world's largest religion and still growing – especially in the American continent and Africa. Since the end of Communism in Russia, numbers have also grown there and more people are becoming Christian in China and Indonesia.

In Europe, however, the number of those going to Christian churches is getting smaller, with fewer people than ever now going to church. In Britain, about 27 per cent of the population go to church regularly. In France, it is 21 per cent and in Sweden it is just 4 per cent.

Islam

There are now Muslims living in almost every country in the world. In more than 50 countries, there are more Muslims than followers of any other religion. These countries stretch from Morocco in North Africa across to the Middle East and further east to Afghanistan and Pakistan. There are also many Muslims in Central Africa, including Nigeria, and also in Indonesia and Russia. In China, there may be as many as 15 million Muslims. Many have settled in European countries – with, for example, about 1.5 million Muslims living in Britain.

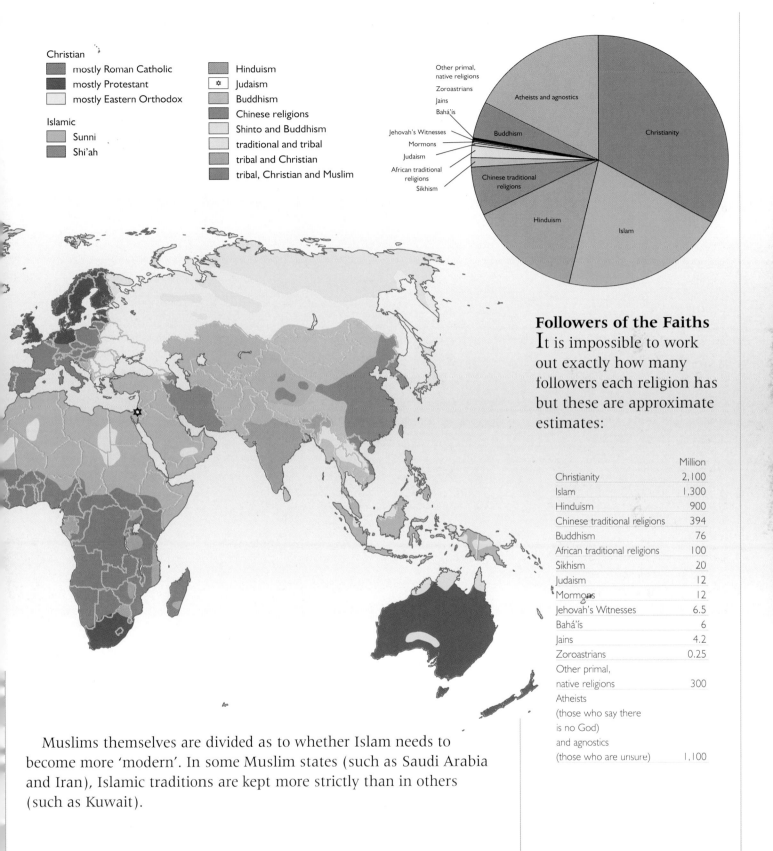

Christian
- mostly Roman Catholic
- mostly Protestant
- mostly Eastern Orthodox

Islamic
- Sunni
- Shi'ah

- Hinduism
- ✿ Judaism
- Buddhism
- Chinese religions
- Shinto and Buddhism
- traditional and tribal
- tribal and Christian
- tribal, Christian and Muslim

Pie chart labels: Other primal, native religions; Zoroastrians; Jains; Bahá'ís; Atheists and agnostics; Jehovah's Witnesses; Mormons; Judaism; African traditional religions; Sikhism; Buddhism; Christianity; Islam; Hinduism; Chinese traditional religions

Followers of the Faiths

It is impossible to work out exactly how many followers each religion has but these are approximate estimates:

	Million
Christianity	2,100
Islam	1,300
Hinduism	900
Chinese traditional religions	394
Buddhism	76
African traditional religions	100
Sikhism	20
Judaism	12
Mormons	12
Jehovah's Witnesses	6.5
Bahá'ís	6
Jains	4.2
Zoroastrians	0.25
Other primal, native religions	300
Atheists (those who say there is no God) and agnostics (those who are unsure)	1,100

Muslims themselves are divided as to whether Islam needs to become more 'modern'. In some Muslim states (such as Saudi Arabia and Iran), Islamic traditions are kept more strictly than in others (such as Kuwait).

Followers of the world's religions have sometimes come into conflict with one another because of rivalry, ignorance or suspicion.

In Modern Times

In recent years, sadly, it has often been the conflicts between groups drawn from the different world faiths that have made the headlines:

In 1992, there was fighting between Hindus and Muslims in Ayodhya in India when some Muslims tried to build a mosque in what they said was a Muslim holy place. Many Hindus said it was the birthplace of their god Rama.

In 1992, civil war began in what was then Yugoslavia. The conflict was made worse by quarrels between different religious faiths.

In 2001, the destruction of the Twin Towers of the World Trade Center in New York, USA, by terrorists caused tension between Christians and Muslims.

Sometimes the tension has been within one faith. From 1969, there was fighting in Northern Ireland between Roman Catholic and Protestant Christians.

Look it Up

59 🌳 Religious Conflict

Both Christianity and Islam are missionary faiths. That is, their followers set out to try to persuade more people to join their way of thinking – and they have sometimes treated those with different views harshly and cruelly.

Christians and Jews

Christians have not always had good relations with the Jewish people. For many centuries, many Christians blamed the Jews for the death of Jesus and treated them as second-class citizens, expelling them from certain countries or forcing them to live in ghettos.

Christians and Native Religions

As Christians explored and conquered parts of the world from the fifteenth century onwards, some of them saw nothing wrong in forcing the original inhabitants of the countries they discovered to become Christian.

Some African women in Namibia still wear the dress of nineteenth-century European missionaries.

Christianity and Islam

As Muslims tried to make countries accept Islam, they sometimes came into conflict with Christianity. These conflicts led to the Crusades and to Muslim rule in Spain for many years. Much later, as the British empire grew and Britain took control of Muslim countries in the Middle East and Asia, there were more outbreaks of trouble. Nowadays, there is again suspicion and even hatred between some followers of these two faiths.

In 1992, a 500-year-old Babri mosque at Ayodha, India, was destroyed by Hindus wanting to build a Hindu temple in its place. In the riots which followed, over 2,000 people were killed. This Indian policeman is guarding statues to be used in a temple.

'No doubt religion has to answer for some of the most terrible crimes in history. But that is the fault not of religion but of … man.'

– Mahatma Gandhi

Jerusalem

Jerusalem is a holy city for members of three religions.

• For Jews...

It is the centre of their 'Promised Land'. It was here that their King David built his capital city. It was here his son, King Solomon, built the first great Temple – and Jerusalem became the centre of Jewish worship.

• For Christians...

It is where the most important events in the life of Jesus took place. It is where he had his last supper with his disciples, where he was put to death on a cross and where his followers believed he rose from the dead three days later.

• For Muslims...

It is their third most important city after Makkah and Madinah. Muslims believe their Prophet visited it on a 'Night Journey', in which he was led to the city where he met Ibrahim (Abraham), Moses and Jesus, and visited heaven.

The word Jerusalem means 'City of Peace'. Sadly, Jerusalem has not always been a peaceful place and has often been fought over. First, the Babylonians and (much later) the Romans forced the Jews to leave their city. Then in the year 638 CE , the city was captured by the second Muslim *khalifah*, Umar. It is said he treated the people then living there well. Four hundred years later, in 1099 CE, Christian armies laid siege to the city, eventually capturing it back from Muslim control. Thousands of people were killed during this 'crusade'.

The Muslims recaptured the city once again in 1187. Their leader, Salah-ad-Din (sometimes known as Saladin), ordered that no Christian should be harmed. Nevertheless, the Crusades continued for almost 200 years as Christians tried to take Jerusalem back under their control.

When the state of Israel was created in 1947, the city was shared between Jews and Arabs. In 1967, the Jews took control of the whole city. There has been continuing violence and tension.

A famous mosque called the Dome of the Rock stands where Solomon's Temple once stood – just beyond the Western Wall of the Temple.

Look it Up

7 The Promised Land
12 Judaism in the Modern World
13 The Man Called Jesus
19 Festivals and Holy Days
22 The Spread of Islam

An aerial view of Temple Mount, Jerusalem, showing the Dome of the Rock.

The Interfaith Movement

As members of different religions get to know each other, they often become more ready to work and live alongside those of different faiths. This has come to be known as the Interfaith Movement.

In 1893, a 'Parliament of the World's Religions' was held in Chicago in the United States of America. Since then, many interfaith meetings and discussions have been held at both international and local levels.

Some of these meetings allow ordinary people to get to know each other. Other meetings involve religious leaders working for world peace and an end to poverty, hunger and unnecessary sickness.

This image, known as a mandala, contains the symbols of some of the major world religions. It is seen here on a building in Kodaikanal, southern India.

60 🌳 Living Together

In recent years, people have started to migrate much more than they used to, leaving one country to live in another – sometimes to find work or to escape a war. For example, there are now Taoists living in the United States of America, Buddhists in Scotland, Hindus in Germany, Muslims in France and Jews in Morocco. The different customs and ways of life and worship can seem very strange to new neighbours. For example:

- Some never cut their hair; others shave their heads.
- Some never cover their heads in their places of worship; others always cover their heads.
- Some worship standing up; others pray while sitting cross-legged.
- Some worship in silence; others sing, dance and wave their arms.

The daily life of a Buddhist in Thailand is very different from that of a Christian in Britain. What matters most to a Hindu in an Indian village is very different to what matters to one in the United States of America. There may be violent conflict between Sunni and Shi'ah Muslims in Iraq. There may be little agreement on certain matters between Roman Catholic and Protestant Christians.

Living Together

There are three ways in which those of different religions can relate to one another.

- By believing that one's own religion is the only true way and that all other religions are false – or even dangerous. This is called 'exclusivism'.
- By believing that there should be one single world religion or to say that what matters is what everyone can agree on. This is called 'inclusivism'.
- By keeping and supporting one's own religion – but to be friendly towards and respectful of other beliefs. This is called 'pluralism' and is the aim of the Interfaith Movement.

The founders, prophets and teachers of all the major world faiths have tried to show the way towards a better future. While their teachings remain distinctive and special to their followers, they have enough in common for people to live in peace with one another and to discover a meaning and purpose for their lives.

The Golden Rule

It has been said that all religions have one teaching in common. In simple words, it is the idea that people should be good to each other. This is sometimes called 'the Golden Rule'.

Christianity: 'Do for others what you want them to do for you.'

Matthew 7:12

Confucianism: 'What you do not want done to you, do not do to others.'

Analects 15.23

Sikhism: 'Do not create enmity with anyone, for God is within everyone.'

Guru Granth Sahib 259

Judaism: 'What is hateful to you, do not do to your fellow human being.'

Talmud, Shabbat 31

Islam: 'No one of you is a believer until he desires for his brother that which he desires for himself.'

Sunnah

Jainism: 'We should regard all creatures as we regard our own self.'

Mahavir

Hinduism: 'Do nothing unto others which would cause you pain if it were done to you.'

Mahabharata 5:1517

Buddhism: 'Hurt not others in ways that you yourself would find hurtful.'

Udana-Varga 5.18

Index